HIKE
GRIFFITH PARK & HOLLYWOOD HILLS

Hike. Contemplate what makes you happy and what makes you happier still. Follow a trail or blaze a new one. **Hike.** Think about what you can do to expand your life and someone else's. **Hike.** Slow down. Gear up. **Hike.** Connect with friends. Re-connect with nature.

Hike. Shed stress. Feel blessed. **Hike** to remember. **Hike** to forget. **Hike** for recovery. **Hike** for discovery. **Hike.** Enjoy the beauty of providence. **Hike.** Share the way, The Hiker's Way, on the long and winding trail we call life.

HIKE GRIFFITH PARK & HOLLYWOOD HILLS

BY
JOHN MCKINNEY

TheTrailmaster.com

HIKE Griffith Park & Hollywood Hills By John McKinney

HIKE Griffith Park & Hollywood Hills © 2019. The Trailmaster, Inc. All rights reserved. Manufactured in the United States of America. No part of this book may be used or reproduced in any manner whatsoever without written permission except in the case of brief quotations embodied in articles and reviews.

ISBN-13: ISBN 978-0934161-76-3

Book Design by Lisa DeSpain
Cartography by Mark Chumley
Cover photo by Dan Waters
HIKE Series Editor: Cheri Rae
Photo Credits: Courtesy of Lionsgate, p. 25; Courtesy of Santa Monica Mountains Conservancy, p. 123.

Published by Olympus Press and The Trailmaster, Inc. www.TheTrailmaster.com (Visit our site for a complete listing of all Trailmaster publications, products, and services.)

Although The Trailmaster, Inc. and the author have made every attempt to ensure that information in this book is accurate, they are not responsible for any loss, damage, injury, or inconvenience that may occur to you while using this information. You are responsible for your own safety; the fact that an activity or trail is described in this book does not mean it will be safe for you. Trail conditions can change from day to day; always check local conditions and know your limitations.

Contents

Introduction 11
Griffith Park 15
Hollywood Hills 21
Hikes to HOLLYWOOD Sign 25

I Griffith Park

FERNDELL 29
   Along a bubbling brook amid redwoods and 50 kinds of ferns

GRIFFITH OBSERVATORY 33
   Pathways to the Planetarium from Ferndell

MT. HOLLYWOOD 37
   Griffith Park's premiere peak and most popular trail

HOLLYWOOD SIGN FROM GRIFFITH OBSERVATORY ... 41
   Two iconic peaks in one fun-packed hike: Mt. Hollywood and Mt. Lee

GLENDALE PEAK 45
   A mile from Mt. Hollywood, a world apart

CEDAR GROVE & VISTA VIEW POINT 49
   Greenery, scenery, and views from a scenic road that's now hikers-only

BEACON HILL 53
    Remembering Grand Central Airport with a pilot's-eye view of L.A.

MT. HOLLYWOOD FROM OLD L.A. ZOO 57
    Day and night, a great way to go

BEE ROCK 61
    Beehive-shaped formation a favorite destination of hikers for 100 years

AMIR'S GARDEN & MOUNT BELL 65
    A hiker's oasis, the trail wisdom of Amir Dialameh, and a mount in the middle of things

WESTERN HERITAGE 69
    Giddy-up! From the Museum of the American West to Travel Town

BRONSON CAVE 73
    Batman's Cave and location for many movies, classic and cheesy

HOLLYWOOD SIGN FROM BRUSH CANYON 77
    Fast becoming the most popular hike to the HOLLYWOOD Sign

II Hollywood Hills

HOLLYWOOD SIGN FROM BEACHWOOD DR 83
    Classic Hollyridge Trail, longtime hiker favorite. (Closed pending resolution of access dispute.)

HOLLYWOOD SIGN FROM INNSDALE DR 87
    Easy hike to Hollywood Sign Overlook, Selfie Heaven!

HOLLYWOOD SIGN FROM WONDERVIEW DR 91
    Cahuenga Peak, Wisdom Tree, and a trail to the HOLLYWOOD Sign for the true hiker

HOLLYWOOD RESERVOIR 95
    Loop around Lake Hollywood with vistas of HOLLYWOOD Sign

RUNYON CANYON 99
   Storied canyon and good hiking steps from Hollywood Blvd.

RUNYON CANYON (NORTH) 103
   From Indian Peak and other overlooks, gain grand metropolitan vistas

WATTLES GARDEN PARK 107
   A bucolic retreat in the heart of Hollywood with trail connections to Runyon Canyon

TREBEK OPEN SPACE 111
   Hike preserve donated by "Jeopardy" host. What is Trebek Park?

III Far Eastern Santa Monica Mountains

WILACRE PARK & COLDWATER CANYON 117
   A tramp across Cross Mountain Park to The TreePeople's domain

FRYMAN CANYON OVERLOOK 121
   Plants, native and not; architecture, sublime and ridiculous; vistas near and far

DIXIE CANYON PARK 124
   Warren Beatty, thank you for this woodsy retreat

BRIAR SUMMIT 126
   An easy hike leads to stellar views from this former Nike Missile Observation Site

UPPER FRANKLIN CANYON 129
   TV and movie producers like it as much as hikers

LOWER FRANKLIN CANYON 133
   Walk on the wild side of Beverly Hills 90210

BEL-AIR 137
   Bel Air-bound Getty View Trail rises high above Sepulveda Pass and offers museum and metropolitan views

ABOUT THE AUTHOR 140

The HOLLYWOOD Sign sure looks different when you're hiking <u>above</u> it!

EVERY TRAIL TELLS A STORY.

> *Work-out hikes, nature hikes, hill climbs. And a wonderful diversity of hikers. Enjoy!*

HIKE ON.

The quiet chaparral hills—famous throughout the world because of the Griffith Observatory and HOLLYWOOD Sign—are for the hiker a quiet retreat from the busy metropolis below.

Introduction

Griffith Park will always have a special place in my heart. I was born in Glendale, only a mile away from the park's eastern boundary. My parents introduced me to park trails at a very tender age; by their recollection, the sojourn to Bee Rock was my first hike.

I have fond memories of hiking Griffith Park in the many years since: as a Boy Scout, during my college days at the University of Southern California, on Sierra Club-led hikes. I introduced my own children to the pleasures of hiking in the park, and have always enjoyed taking out-of-town guests from across the country and around the world up to Mt. Hollywood and of course the HOLLYWOOD Sign.

During my 18-year stint as the *Los Angeles Times* hiking columnist, I often wrote stories about Griffith Park trails and these accounts proved to be among the most popular with readers.

Hiking Griffith Park and the Hollywood Hills has been a favorite pastime for Angelenos for more than 100 years. By some accounts, members of the

Sierra Club's Angeles Chapter have been leading hikes in Griffith Park since the 1940s.

Many of the park's most colorful figures have praised the wonders of this natural haven in the midst of the metropolis. It was an honor and a privilege for me to walk with and talk with Griffith Park legends Charlie Turner (Dante Orgolini's longtime successor as caretaker of Dante's View) and botanist-ranger-historian extraordinaire Bill Eckert. I'll always remember the founder of Amir's Garden, Amir Dialameh, who lived by the motto: "In the land of the free, plant a tree."

Outside the boundaries of Griffith Park, several other locales in the Hollywood Hills beckon the hiker. "Hollywood Hills," the affluent neighborhood, measures just seven square miles, but the hills available for hiking are much more extensive.

The Hollywood Hills are known to millions around the world for the presence of the HOLLYWOOD sign. Many tourists, hikers and not, mistakenly believe the iconic landmark rests atop Mt. Hollywood in Griffith Park rather than on the summit of nearby Mt. Lee outside the park. I always enjoy the smiles on the faces of visitors as they make the pilgrimage to the top of the sign.

Along with the natural attractions and more than 100 miles of hiking trails, I'm attracted to Griffith Park and the Hollywood Hills for three more

Introduction

reasons: the variety of vistas, the connection to the film industry and the diversity of hikers met along the way.

The summit of Mt. Hollywood (1,625 feet) provides an extraordinary vantage point for clear-day views of Mt. Lee and the bold HOLLYWOOD lettering across its summit, plus the entire Los Angeles Basin from the San Gabriel Mountains to the Pacific Ocean. I love the views from Beacon Hill, Glendale Peak, Fryman Overlook and Inspiration Point atop Runyon Canyon.

Ever since pioneer silent filmmaker D.W. Griffith (no relation to park founder Colonel Griffith J. Griffith) filmed the battle scenes for his epic "Birth of a Nation" in the park in 1915, Griffith Park has been a popular location for movies. Annually, Griffith Park is often the busiest destination in Los Angeles for on-location filming.

The park has a lot of different "looks"—and with moviemaker magic can be made to mimic locales around the world. By now, virtually every nook and cranny in the park has appeared in a commercial, film or TV show.

For film fans, it's fun to hike past Griffith Observatory and recall scenes from "The Terminator" or that 1955 James Dean classic, "Rebel Without a Cause." Or hike to and through Bronson Caves, used in that campy sci-fi flick, "Invasion of the Body Snatchers," the John Wayne western, "The Searchers," and as the Bat Cave in the Batman TV series of the 1960s. The HOLLYWOOD Sign has been featured in dozens of films, beginning with "Hollywood Boulevard" in 1935 and including "The Day of the Locust," "The Italian Job," "Earthquake" and "Shrek II."

I'm also delighted by the number of new hikers I meet on the trail: on work-out hikes in Wilacre Park, on nature hikes in Franklin Canyon, on hill climbs to Bee Rock, Cahuenga Peak and Getty View. And it's wonderful to see such a diversity of hikers—of all ages, colors and ethnic backgrounds.

Hike smart, reconnect with nature and have a wonderful time on the trail.

Hike on.

—John McKinney

Griffith Park

There really are two Griffith Parks. One is the familiar urban park with landscaped shrubbery, golf courses, picnic areas, museums, observatory and zoo. The other is a wild park—mountain country—with 53 miles of trail to explore.

Geography

The 4,310-acre park forms the eastern terminus of the Santa Monica Mountains and offers the hiker a taste of the range's cliffs and crags. The mountains—usually called the Hollywood Hills on this eastern end—extend between Los Feliz and Burbank and include the park's famed high point 1,625-foot Mt. Hollywood.

The Hollywood Hills are more often associated with fine homes than with fine hikes. Depending on who's dividing up the hills into residential areas, neighborhoods include Beachwood Canyon, Hollywood Dell, Mt. Olympus, Sunset Hills and Outpost Estates, and might also include Coldwater Canyon, Fryman Canyon and Laurel Canyon.

The park is surrounded on three sides by freeways: the Hollywood Freeway on the west, the Ventura Freeway on the north and the Golden State Freeway on the east. A more natural boundary (particularly after recent ecological restoration efforts) is the Los Angeles River, which borders the park east and north.

Two-thirds of the park, one of North America's largest urban parks (attracting an estimated 10 million visitors annually), is rugged, undeveloped mountain country.

Natural Attractions

The park shares a common flora and fauna with the rest of the Santa Monica Mountains to the west. Most hillsides are covered with chaparral—chamise, ceanothus, toyon and buckwheat. Poppies, bush lupine, and the occasional wild purple onion splash color around the park. The brushy slopes of the park, burned in a 2007 fire, are recovering well, particularly the native coastal scrub and chaparral communities.

Canyon bottoms are shaded with oak and sycamore. Planted pines and eucalyptus groves are scattered on hill and dale. More than a hundred tree species grow in the park; this diversity contributes to a wide variety of bird life, numbering more than a hundred species as well.

The park has a few botanical surprises including ferns in Fern Canyon and a grove of redwoods in Ferndell.

Lovingly tended gardens—Amir's Garden and Dante's View—are hilltop oases that delight plant lovers.

History

Park founder Colonel Griffith J. Griffith, a colorful character indeed.

Colonel Griffith Jenkins Griffith, a Welshman who made fortunes in gold mining and Los Angeles real estate astonished the city when he presented it with 3,000 acres for a park in 1896. Many resented his philanthropy however, suggesting Griffith's gift was merely a ruse to dodge taxes.

In 1903 Griffith lost more of the citizenry's respect when he stood trial for the attempted murder of his wife. Convicted, he served two years in San Quentin Prison, and came back to Los Angeles, still trying to prove his civic spirit. He offered the city $100,000 for an observatory, but the city refused. Only after Griffith's death in 1919 did the city take the Colonel's money, in order to build the observatory and Greek Theater.

Eventually the city built golf courses, picnic grounds and a zoo. During the Depression of the 1930s, thousands of workers built the park's road and trail system. A 1933 brush fire in the Mineral Wells Area claimed the lives of 36 workmen—in terms of loss of life, the most disastrous fire in the history of Los Angeles.

Following Griffith's original gift of parkland, city purchases and private donations have helped expand the park. In 1944, the Sherman Company donated 444 acres surrounding the HollywoodLand development to Griffith Park. In 2010, a star studded cast of donors from the film industry purchased 100 acres or so around Cahuenga Peak to add to the park.

Griffith Park's rugged terrain has long been a favorite and convenient location for filmmakers. Year after year, the park ranks among the most popular film locations in Los Angeles.

Administration

Griffith Park is under the stewardship of the City of Los Angles Department of Recreation and Parks, laparks.org, 323-665-3051.

"Friends" groups include the Los Angeles Parks Foundation (laparksfoundation.org), Friends of the Observatory (griffithobservatory.org) and Friends of Griffith Park (friendsofgriffithpark.org).

Famed Griffith Observatory attracts more than a million visitors a year from all over the world.

Griffith Observatory: Essential Info for Hikers

A must-see attraction for visitors from around the world, Griffith Observatory is also a destination for hikers; nearby is Charlie Turner Trailhead, starting point for trails leading to Mt. Hollywood—and throughout the park. Hikers can drive to the Observatory (paid parking); take low-cost public transit; take a hike from other locales and (free) places to park.

Paid Parking Near the Observatory: The Observatory parking lot, as well as parking on West Observatory Road and on Western Canyon Road require payment on Monday–Friday 12 noon to 10:00 P.M. and Saturday–Sunday 10 A.M. to 10 P.M. Parking fees range from $6 to $10 per hour; pay stations accept only credit cards. After parking, go to a pay station and carefully follow the instructions. Take your paid receipt back to your vehicle and place it on the dashboard. Vehicles not displaying a receipt will get a parking citation.

Transit: Reach the Observatory via DASH bus service from the Vermont/Sunset Metro Red Line station to the Observatory during the following times: Monday–Friday 12 noon to 10 p.m; Saturday–Sunday 10 A.M. to 10 P.M. The bus arrives at the front of the Observatory every 20 to 25 minutes, with stops along the way at Mt. Hollywood Drive (access to hiking trails), the Greek Theatre (access to hiking trails), and on Hillhurst Avenue in Los Feliz Village. Cost is 50 cents, less or free for various transit pass holders.

Park Free and Hike a Mile: Parking is free in the areas around the Greek Theatre and Fern Dell. It's about a one-mile hike from these trailheads to the Observatory.

Hollywood Hills

The quiet chaparral hills—famous throughout the world because of the HOLLYWOOD Sign—are for the hiker a quiet retreat from the busy metropolis below.

Geography

The Hollywood Hills are the eastern end of the Santa Monica Mountains and share a similar ecology to the range's taller and wilder peaks to the west. The differences between the two ends of the range have more to do with human settlement than natural history; the Hollywood Hills are by far the most developed part of the mountains.

Where do the Hollywood Hills "end" and the Santa Monica Mountains begin? Certainly there's no firm boundary. The hills above Beverly Hills and Bel Air, as well as Franklin and Coldwater Canyons, literally and figuratively have a Hollywood connection. Griffith Park encompasses the easternmost part of the Hollywood Hills.

The Hollywood Hills separate the San Fernando Valley from Hollywood, Beverly Hills and parts of Los Angeles. They present a dramatic picture from afar, not because of their height (800 to 1,820 feet), but because the steep canyons of the hills makes them look particularly rugged.

Natural History

"Living in the Hollywood Hills" has long implied living in a locale favored by celebrities—and also living close to nature. Ringed by busy freeways and high-trafficked boulevards, the hills nevertheless remain a semi-natural retreat.

Hillsides are covered by the chaparral and coastal sage scrub communities including chamise, California buckwheat, manzanita and many more Mediterranean and drought-tolerant flora. Coyotes, rabbits, deer, squirrels, and raccoons are frequently sighted in the hills.

During the holiday season, the rich green crown of the toyon bush is aglow with a mass of red berries. Toyon—also known variously as Christmas berry or California holly—is the most festive of flora. Masses of this native shrub growing on the hills above Hollywood gave the community its name.

History

Anthropological evidence suggests that the Chumash occupied the Santa Monica Mountains as far east as Topanga Canyon and the land we now call the Hollywood Hills was occupied by Shoshonean-speaking people. The most eastern part of the hills was occupied by the Gabrielinos.

During California's Spanish and Mexican rule, the hills were considered of little value. Ranches were located down in the valley and property lines extended into higher terrain.

Until the beginning of the 20th century, the population of Hollywood numbered only about 500; deer ventured down to Hollywood Boulevard in the early morning and evening hours. When the moviemakers came, Hollywood's flatlands and hills were settled.

The HOLLYWOODLAND Sign was constructed in 1923 to promote a housing development.

Hollywood, the city, has had its share of urban problems, but the name "Hollywood" endures as a synonym for the TV and motion picture industries. And the HOLLYWOOD Sign, perched on Mt. Lee, is the most easily identified symbol for the entertainment industry.

Preservation of parks and preserves in the Hollywood Hills is inextricably linked to the entertainment industry as well. Alex Trebek, host of the popular game show "Jeopardy!" donated land for a preserve adjacent to Runyon Canyon. In 2010 Hollywood notables such as Steven Spielberg and Tom Hanks pitched in to purchase Cahuenga Peak for parkland.

Administration

Mountain Recreation and Conservation Authority manages Coldwater Canyon, Fryman Canyon, and Wilacre parks (lamountains.com). Runyon Canyon is managed by the City of Los Angeles Department of Recreation and Parks and Franklin Canyon by the National Park Service.

Hikes to the Hollywood Sign

HOLLYWOOD Sign from Griffith Observatory: Visit two iconic peaks, Mt. Hollywood and Mt. Lee on this longer hike.

HOLLYWOOD Sign from Brush Canyon: Visit the Bronson Caves ("Bat Cave"), ascend Brush Canyon to Mulholland Trail, then over to Mt. Lee Drive to the sign.

HOLLYWOOD Sign from Innsdale Drive: Easy hike to Hollywood Sign Overlook (Selfie Heaven), followed by ascent on Mulholland Trail and Mt. Lee Drive to the sign.

HOLLYWOOD Sign from Wonderview Drive: A somewhat challenging route for the true hiker! Visit the Wisdom Tree, and ascend Burbank Peak and Cahuenga Peak via Aileen Getty Trail on the way to the Sign.

HOLLYWOOD Sign from Beachwood Canyon Drive: Classic Hollyridge Trail closed pending resolution of access dispute.

You can also hike to the HOLLYWOOD Sign from several popular locales in Griffith Park including Ferndell, Griffith Observatory, and Mt. Hollywood. Trailmaster recommendation: Climbing to Mt. Hollywood AND to the HOLLYWOOD Sign on the slopes of Mt. Lee adds up to a great hike!

Discover more hikes at TheTrailmaster.com

Many scenes from the 2017 blockbuster musical "La La Land" were filmed in Griffith Park.

EVERY TRAIL TELLS A STORY.

I
GRIFFITH PARK

HIKE ON.

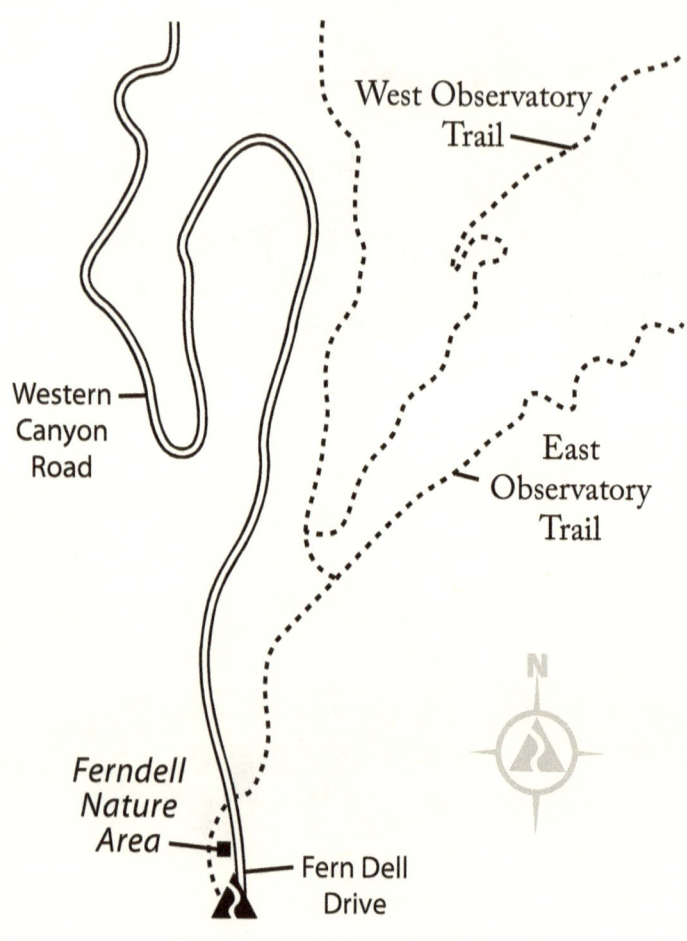

Ferndell

Ferndell Trail

From Western Canyon entrance to upper Ferndell is 0.5 mile round trip

In well-named Ferndell, a brook bubbles through a woodsy, fern-lined glen. The brook waters redwoods that thrive at the bottom of the dell. Native sycamore and alder also shade this oasis located at the Western Canyon entrance of Griffith Park.

Not surprisingly, this tropical garden is a popular TV and film location. More than 50 varieties of ferns thrive in the dell, along with other flowering plants and lush vegetation. The brook attracts numerous birds including brown towhees, robins and jays. (Until the Observatory was renovated in 2006, recycled water from the cooling system was sent merrily on its way down to the dell.)

The path through lush and shady Ferndell is a park favorite, particularly on a hot day. I remember taking my kids on a walk through Ferndell in the rain. They loved it. Magic!

The official park website calls it "Ferndell Nature Museum." No building here, though. On the map it's "Ferndell Nature Area." You half expect a nature trail brochure or interpretive signs.

You might notice that my spelling of Ferndell differs from the predominant spelling ("Fern Dell") found in print and online media. The Trailmaster has reasons for being contrary.

Some years ago I hiked with L.A. City Councilman Tom LaBonge ("Mr. Griffith Park") who said he goes with the classic, old-school spelling of Ferndell as one word, because that's its historic use. I remember, going all the way back to my Boy Scout days, Ferndell as one word. I've also heard that Ferndell is run together as one word to help distinguish it from the Fern Canyon (most definitely two words) area of the park.

L.A. Times style, during my long hiking columnist tenure there, was to use Ferndell as one word. Bolstering the case for one word is the onetime Ferndell Ranger Station (now removed) and geologists who long ago identified a fault in this area of the park, still known as the Ferndell Fault.

After you emerge from the greenery of lower Ferndell, make your way through upper Ferndell and its picnic grounds to join a pathway to Griffith Observatory (see hike description).

DIRECTIONS: From Los Feliz Boulevard, one block east of Western Avenue, turn north on Fern Dell Drive and proceed just 0.1 mile to the signed entrance to Ferndell on your left. Park along Fern Dell Drive.

THE HIKE: What a beautiful trailhead! It's landscaped in stone with a wooden sign that proclaims "Ferndell." Stroll through the gate into the streamside sanctuary.

Meander the historic pathway lined with stone retaining walls. Old-fashioned handrails and footbridges, as well as benches placed in contemplative spots, add to this classic walk in the park.

About a quarter-mile from the start, the pathway curves right, leads under Fern Dell Drive and, all too soon, it's *finis* for Ferndell. To continue to Griffith Observatory, walk past the restrooms and, keeping the brook on your left, follow the path that curves right (east).

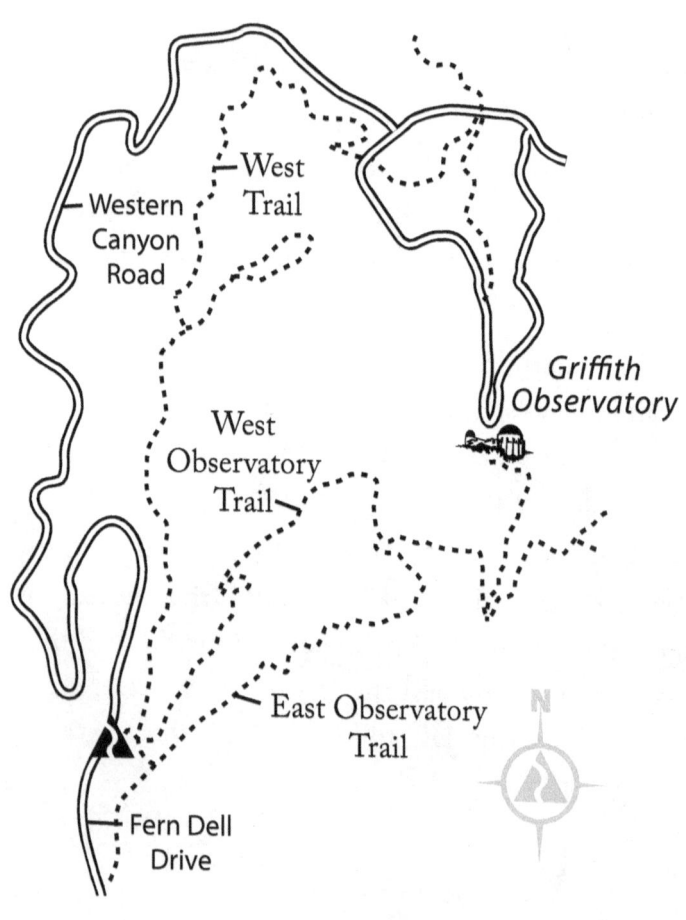

TheTrailmaster.com

Griffith Observatory

East and West Observatory Trails

From Ferndell to Griffith Observatory is 2.4 miles round trip with 500-foot elevation gain

Griffith Observatory opened to the public in 1935 and has been an L.A. cultural institution, tourist attraction, and L.A. landmark in every sense of the word ever since. The observatory has been featured in many films including that James Dean classic, "Rebel Without a Cause," as well as "The Terminator" and "Transformers."

The observatory, planetarium and extensive array of space and science exhibits, combined with lectures by leading astronomers and scientists, have interpreted the wonders of the universe for generations of schoolchildren and an enthusiastic public. Closed in 2002 for an extensive $93 million renovation, the observatory reopened in 2006, retaining its Art Deco exterior and adding all new exhibits, the Leonard

Nimoy Event Horizon Theater and Café at the End of the Universe. The 2007 Griffith Park Fire came dangerously close to Griffith Observatory.

This hike crosses upper Ferndell and joins West Observatory Trail for a climb up the south-facing slope of Mt. Hollywood to the observatory. Hikers get vistas of the L.A. Basin from downtown to the Pacific Ocean. Extend this hike by continuing to the top of Mt. Hollywood (see hike description) or by beginning in lower Ferndell (see hike description).

Like other stellar stargazing destinations you can reach by road or trail such as Mt. Wilson and Palomar Mountain, you can opt to drive or hike to Griffith Observatory. I say, "take a hike!" You'll get a great workout, special vistas of greater L.A. and the HOLLYWOOD Sign and avoid the ordeal of finding a place to park near the observatory—which attracts more than a million visitors a year.

West Observatory Trail and East Observatory Trail (aka Upper Observatory Trail and Lower Observatory Trail on some maps) ascend from the canyon. Both have much to offer and you take both to make a semi-loop hike. The upper trail (West Observatory) is 0.2 mile longer and gains more elevation).

DIRECTIONS: From Los Feliz Boulevard, one block east of Western Avenue, turn north on Fern Dell Drive and proceed about 0.4 mile and park along the road near the Trails Café, and a junction with Red Oak Drive.

THE HIKE: Join the first trail on your right, East Observatory Trail, and after just a few hundred feet of hiking, look left and note a bridge that crosses a creek and connects to West Observatory Trail.

Begin your ascent and very soon the Observatory pops into view. After angling north, the lower trail East Observatory Trail meets the upper West Observatory Trail and the two proceed in tandem southeast to a vista point and trail junction.

Take a seat on a strategically placed bench and take in the views of the metropolis. Ahead, note the continuation of East Observatory Trail, which descends to Vermont Canyon Road near the Greek Theater. Take the left wide trail onward and upward north 0.2 mile to the eastern end of the observatory.

The trail leads along a wall then over to the lawn on the north side of the observatory. From here you can enter the famed attraction or walk across the parking lot to the trailhead for the hike to Mt. Hollywood.

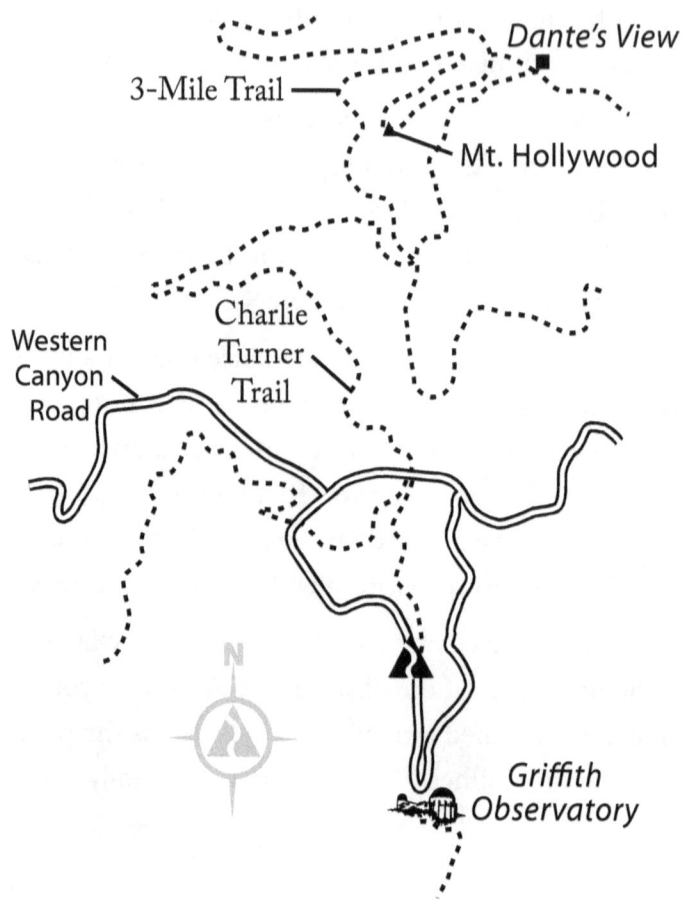

MT. HOLLYWOOD

MT. HOLLYWOOD TRAIL

From Griffith Observatory to Mt. Hollywood is 3 miles round trip with 500-foot elevation gain

Griffith Park's best-known hike leads to the top of 1,625-foot Mt. Hollywood, the park's premiere peak. Mt. Hollywood is not the mountain crowned by the historic Hollywood sign; however, the trail to it delivers great views of Mt. Lee and the bold HOLLYWOOD lettering across its summit. Mt. Hollywood can be hiked by way of several different trails (The Trailmaster's favorites are included in this book) but the route from Griffith Observatory is by far the most popular.

While not the tallest peak in the park, it offers great vistas. On clear days the entire basin is spread out before you from the San Gabriel Mountains to the Pacific Ocean. Sometimes mounts San Gorgonio, Baldy and San Jacinto can be seen. The view at night can be spectacular, too.

The hardest part of this hike might be deciding where to begin—or finding a place to park! Because of the challenging (and sometimes nightmarish) parking situation at the Observatory (see "Observatory Parking" page for info and transit options), consider hiking up to the from Ferndell/Western Canyon.

One good option is West Observatory Trail (1.2 miles to the Observatory). Another good way to go is via West Trail, which ascends from Western Canyon Road to meet Mt. Hollywood Trail at a point 0.2 mile from the Charlie Turner Trailhead.

Artist-writer Dante Orgolini, an immigrant of Italian descent, began planting a two-acre retreat of pine, palm and pepper trees high on the south-facing slope of Mt. Hollywood in 1965. British-born retired insurance agent Charlie Turner took over as caretaker in 1978 after Orgolini's death and, for the next 15 years, until he was nearly 90, hiked to the garden virtually every morning to tend the plants. The trailhead for Mt. Hollywood is named for Turner.

DIRECTIONS: From Los Feliz Boulevard, take Vermont Avenue into the park. Follow signs to Griffith Observatory. Park in the lot or as close as you can to Charlie Turner Trailhead. A low-cost weekend shuttle bus runs to the observatory from stops at the Greek Theatre, or from Hillhurst Avenue and from Los Feliz Boulevard.

THE HIKE: Ascend wide Mt. Hollywood Trail along the narrow ridgeline dividing Vermont Canyon to the east and Western Canyon on the west. Pass planted pines and a junction with West Trail, and then by the Mt. Hollywood Tunnel that connects Western Canyon Road with Vermont Canyon Road. Early on, you'll get views of the HOLLYWOOD Sign.

A mile from the start, reach a major junction. Continue your ascent on the wide fire road to Dante's View, where a water fountain and picnic tables suggest a rest stop for hikers.

Enjoy the vistas and lovely garden and join East Ridge Trail for a short (0.1 mile) ascent to a 4-way junction on the north side of Mt. Hollywood. Go left here for the 0.2-mile climb to the summit of Mt. Hollywood. Along with the 360-degree panoramic vistas from the mountains to the metropolis to the sea, you'll also get a view of—you guessed it—the HOLLYWOOD Sign.

Head back down to the 4-way junction. Return the way you came or descend the western loop of the Mt. Hollywood Trail past Captain's Roost, then connect with the eastern leg of the trail and retrace your steps back to the trailhead.

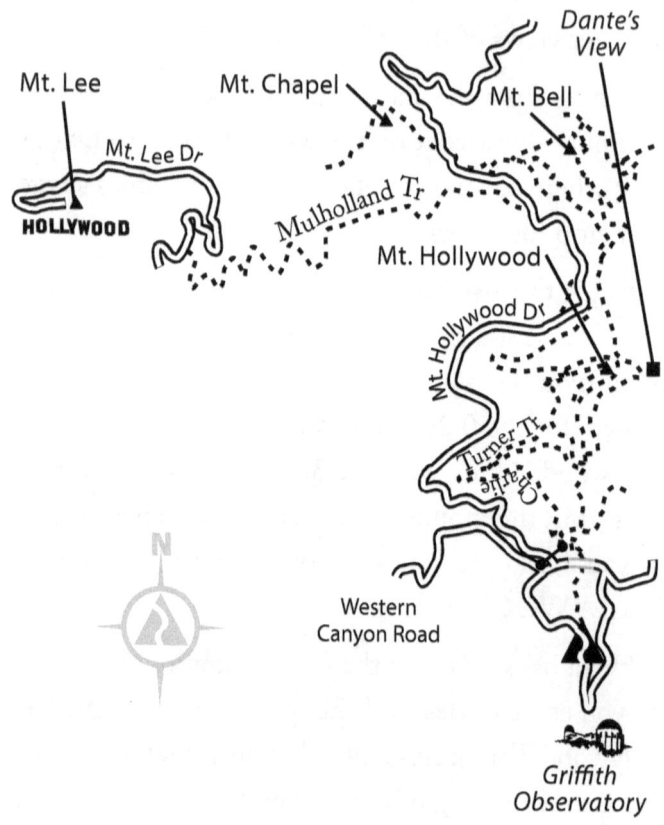

HOLLYWOOD SIGN FROM GRIFFITH OBSERVATORY

Mt. Hollywood, East Ridge, Mulholland, Mt. Lee Trails

From Griffith Observatory to the HOLLYWOOD Sign is 9.2 miles round trip with 600- foot elevation gain

You want it all: Griffith Observatory, Mt. Hollywood, the HOLLYWOOD Sign. And you want to visit all three world-renowned, sights-to-see on one day hike. This then is the hike for you.

It's not the hike for you if you're looking for the most direct route to the HOLLYWOOD Sign. Several other trailheads and trails offer easier and quicker access to the top of Mt. Lee and photo ops of the sign. In fact, you could take the classic hike from the Observatory to Mt. Hollywood AND a second hike to the HOLLYWOOD Sign from another trailhead and the combined total mileage traveled would be less than that of this one hike.

Still determined to go the long way? Good!

The HOLLYWOOD Sign is a hike to remember, but does present a challenge or two. While the point-to-point elevation gain is, as advertised, 600 feet (a tad less, actually), there's a mountain in the middle, so you have two ups and downs.

I strongly recommend an early start because the Griffith Observatory lot and nearby roadside parking fills up fast. Check out all the parking and shuttle options in advance. You want a stress-free start to your great day on the trail.

DIRECTIONS: Locate well-signed Charlie Turner Trailhead at the edge of the Griffith Observatory main lot.

THE HIKE: Ascend wide Mt. Hollywood Trail past planted pines, past a junction with West Trail, and by the Mt. Hollywood Tunnel that connects Western Canyon Road with Vermont Canyon Road. Early on, you'll get views of the HOLLYWOOD Sign.

A mile from the start, reach a 6-way junction. Continue your ascent on the wide fire road to Dante's View. Enjoy the vistas and lovely garden and join East Ridge Trail for a short (0.1 mile) ascent to a 4-way junction on the north side of Mt. Hollywood. Go left here for the 0.2-mile climb to the summit of Mt. Hollywood. Along with the 360-degree panoramic vistas from the mountains to the metropolis to the sea, you'll also get a view of—you guessed it—the HOLLYWOOD Sign.

Return to the 4-way junction. Join Three Mile Trail, which leads 0.6 mile to Mt. Hollywood Drive (a park road closed to vehicles). Turn right and ascend 0.3 mile to a junction with Mulholland Trail (a wide fire road).

Turn left and head west, hiking past junctions with Brush Canyon Trail and Hollyridge Trail (the two classic routes to the HOLLYWOOD Sign). Speaking of the Sign, you'll be getting intermittent and ever changing perspectives on the HOLLYWOOD letters en route—not that you had any doubt you were heading in the right direction!

Mulholland Trail leads to paved Mt. Lee Road, where you turn right and hike a last mile to the top. Near the summit, pass a trail coming up from Cahuenga Peak (yet another route and great hike to the HOLLYWOOD Sign).

Walk along a fence (that keeps visitors from actually getting close to the Sign and obscures the view of it) and join a dirt path to the peak. Awesome views and photo ops galore! Return the same way or select a slightly different route around Mt. Hollywood back to Griffith Observatory and the trailhead.

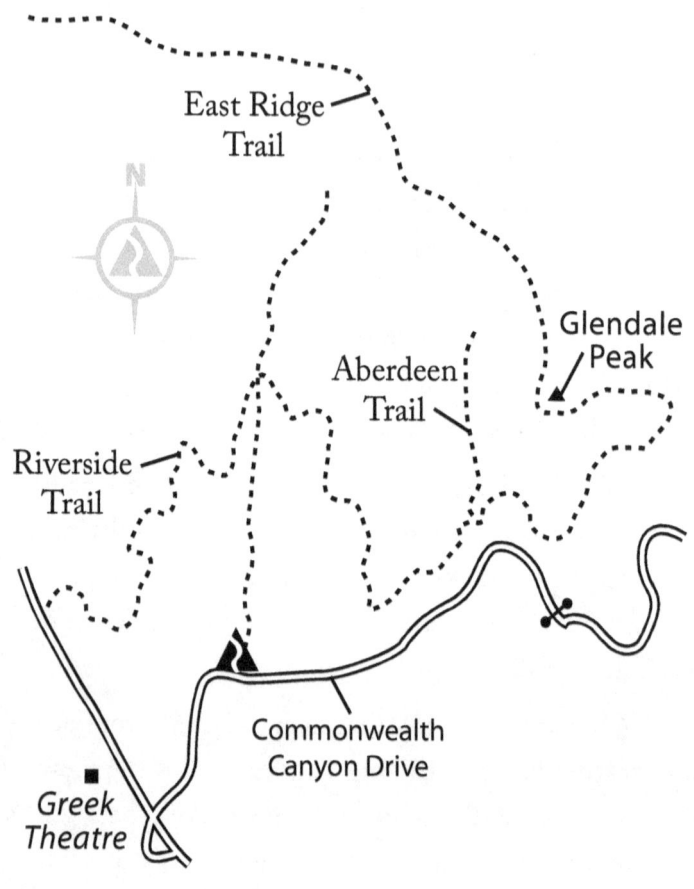

GLENDALE PEAK

RIVERSIDE, HENRY'S TRAILS

To Glendale Peak is 2.6 miles round trip with 500-foot elevation gain

What Glendale Peak lacks in name recognition, it makes up in terrific, clear-day vistas: downtown L.A., Glendale of course, plus panoramas from the San Gabriel Valley to the sea. This Glendale-born hiker likes to climb Glendale Peak on occasion in order to check out the old hometown.

Located literally and figuratively in the shadow of world famous Mt. Hollywood, Glendale Peak (elevation 1,184 feet) is an overlooked destination ignored by all but a handful of hikers. Some maps don't even show the peak, located about one mile east of Mt. Hollywood in the southeast corner of the park.

What little recognition Glendale Peak enjoys comes from efforts of the late, popular Sierra Club hike leader Henry Shamma, who delighted in guiding groups to the summit and sharing the fabulous views. In recognition of Shamma's efforts to maintain the park's gardens and trails, grateful Sierra Club members and park officials dedicated "Henry's Trail," a pathway that leads to Glendale Peak.

DIRECTIONS: Exit the Hollywood Freeway on Vermont Avenue and head north a couple of miles to Los Feliz Boulevard. Continue north on what becomes Vermont Canyon Road for 0.7 mile to Commonwealth Canyon Drive. Turn right and drive 0.2 mile east to the signed entrance for the Vermont Canyon Tennis Facility on the left. Park in the lot below the courts.

THE HIKE: Ascend north on a trail between the tennis courts for a quarter mile to meet unsigned Riverside Trail. Go right on the wide path, which bends south, then east again. The trail dips into Aberdeen Canyon and you'll pass Aberdeen Trail, a narrow spur trail on the left that heads north into the canyon.

Riverside Trail angles northeast and ascends to meet paved Vista Del Valle Drive about a mile from the trailhead. Join East Ridge (Hogback) Trail and begin a clockwise circle of Glendale Peak. From a metal bridge atop Aberdeen Canyon, enjoy vistas of Beacon Hill and beyond along the east side of the park. To reach Glendale Peak, ascend signed Henry's Trail along the summit ridge 0.1 mile south to the top.

Extend your hike with a Trailmaster favorite, East Ridge Trail (Hogback Trail) and tackle the narrow ridge leading up to Dante's View and the shoulder of Mt. Hollywood.

For a different return route, retrace your steps to Vista Valle Drive (closed to vehicles) and head southeast (right) to the redundantly named Vista View Point, a helicopter landing spot. Pass junctions with two trails leading northeast to famed 5-Points; from here you can hike into Fern Canyon or up to Beacon Hill.

The road turns south, curves past Cedar Grove, a popular location for film and TV productions, and meanders west near the park's Nursery and Horticultural Center to meet Commonwealth Canyon Drive. Turn right (north) and follow this road (closed to vehicles on its south end) around the perimeter of Roosevelt Municipal Golf Course back to the tennis courts and trailhead.

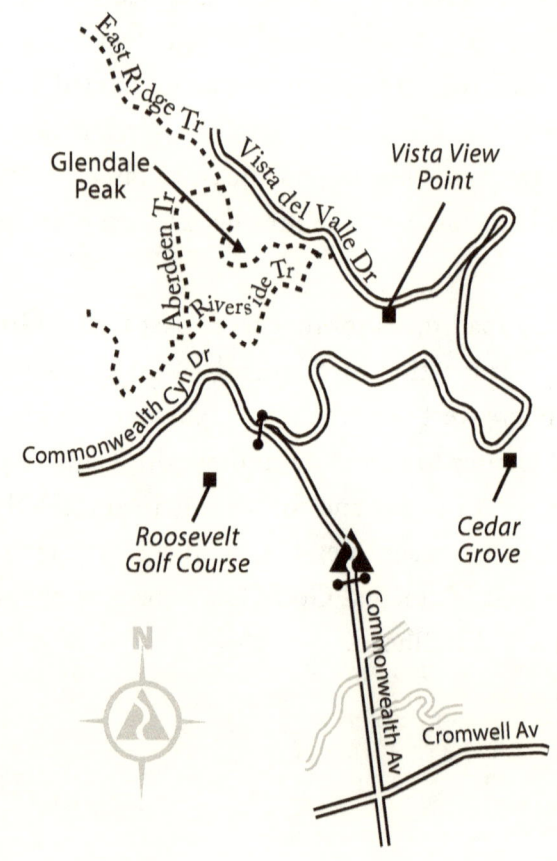

CEDAR GROVE AND VISTA VIEW POINT

VISTA DEL VALLE DRIVE, CEDAR GROVE & VISTA VIEW TRAILS

Loop to Cedar Grove and Vista View Point is 2.6 miles round trip with 400-foot gain

Unlike Mt. Hollywood and Griffith Observatory, Cedar Grove and Vista View Point are way off the tourist track. The greenery, the scenery, and the views from this side of the park are enjoyed mainly by Los Feliz locals or by hikers bound for Glendale Peak and other eastside destinations. Cedar Grove and Vista View Point (like virtually all the other locations in the park!) are often used by film and TV production companies.

More than two-thirds of this short loop hike takes place on asphalt, but fear not; the route is along a scenic (and closed to auto traffic) road that meanders through the east side of the park. Vista del Valle Drive was constructed in the 1930s by Civilian Conservation Corps workers. The impressive stonework along the drive is a reminder of the high quality of the CCC projects completed in Griffith Park during the Great Depression era.

In response to an increase in graffiti, trash dumping and other misbehaviors along Vista del Valle Drive during the 1970s and 80s, park authorities closed the Drive to vehicle traffic in 1992. "View of the Valley" is full of cracks and potholes, but the road's condition is of little concern to the walkers and cyclists who enjoy traveling the now quiet and peaceful byway.

Highpoints, literally and figuratively, for this walk in the park are handsome Cedar Grove and Vista View Point, the latter formerly a super-sized automobile turnout (and now a helipad) that offers wide panoramas from the Griffith Observatory to Hollywood to downtown Los Angeles.

DIRECTIONS: From I-5, exit on Los Feliz Boulevard Exit and head west 1.3 miles to Commonwealth Avenue. Turn right, drive 0.4 miles or so, and park near the top of the road.

THE HIKE: Note the handsome brick and stonework to the right, and walk around the road barrier and up the avenue. Pass Roosevelt Golf Course and meet Vista Del Valle Drive at a signed junction in 0.2 miles. Turn right and begin a mellow ascent.

About 0.75 mile along, as the road curves left, look right for signed Cedar Grove Trail. Loop around the shady grove, partake of the metropolitan views, and return to Vista Del Valle Drive. Turn right and resume your ascent, which takes you past a large water tank painted with a serene forest scene.

Reward to hikers for the climb are more city vistas to the south and east. At a hairpin turn in the road, reach Joe Klass Water Stop, a small picnic area with tables and water for all travelers: a drinking fountain for hikers, horse watering trough for equestrians, stainless steel bowls for canine companions. Note a right-forking trail that leads toward Five Points Junction and Beacon Hill.

Proceed on the road to its crest and impossible-to-miss Vista View Point. Enjoy grand vistas of Hollywood, the Los Feliz and Silverlake neighborhoods, as well as downtown Los Angeles. To the west lie Griffith Observatory and the Greek Theater, and to the northwest Mt. Hollywood and adjacent peaks.

Continue briefly north on Vista Del Valle to intersect two left-forking trails at a well-signed junction. Take the first left (Riverside Trail), and descend the wide dirt trail 0.3 mile into Aberdeen Canyon. As the trail levels out then begins to rise, go left on a short pathway that drops to Commonwealth Canyon Drive.

Go left. In 0.1 mile pass a junction with Vista Del Valle Drive and retrace your steps 0.2 mile back down Commonwealth Canyon Drive to where you began the hike.

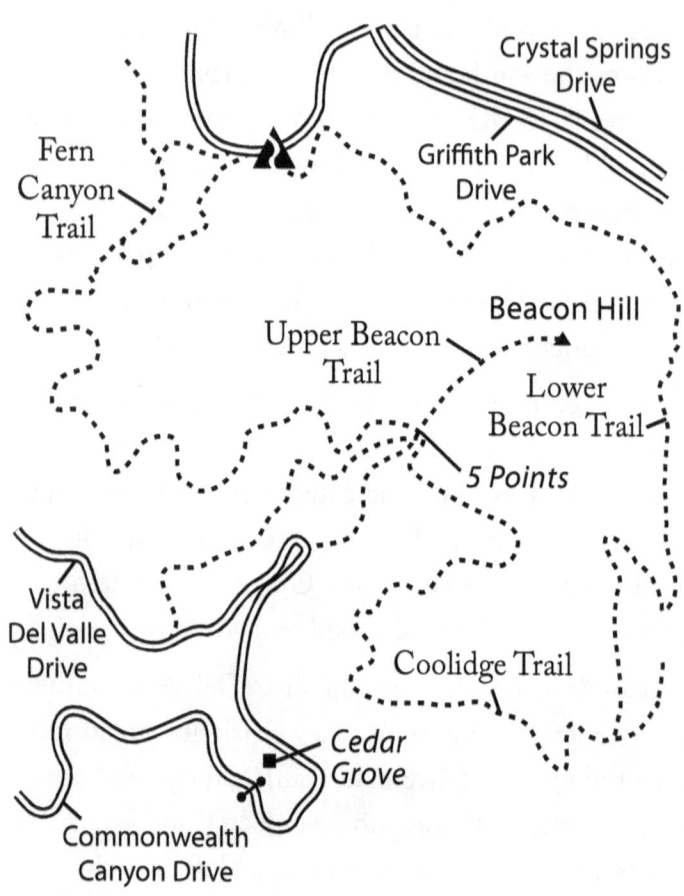

Beacon Hill

Fern Canyon, Upper Beacon, Coolidge and Lower Beacon Trails

4-mile loop around Beacon Hill with 600-foot elevation gain

Long before Los Angeles International Airport was constructed, and in the early days of commercial aviation, Glendale's Grand Central Airport was the Southland's main terminal. In the early years of the 20th century, planes took off from runways next to San Fernando Road.

Atop Beacon Hill was a beacon, illuminated at night to warn approaching aircraft of the high Hollywood Hills near the airport. The beacon is long gone, but you can still get a pilot's-eye-view of Los Angeles from the summit of Beacon Hill.

Beacon Hill (1,001 feet) is the easternmost hill in the Hollywood Hills and easternmost summit in the Santa Monica Mountains that extend 60 miles west to Point Mugu. Auto traffic is a major part of the view from the hilltop these days: the Pasadena, Golden State and Ventura Freeways, plus hundreds of streets and boulevards.

DIRECTIONS: From the Golden State Freeway (I-5) just north of downtown Los Angeles, exit on Los Feliz Boulevard and head west a short ways to Griffith Park's Crystal Springs Drive. Turn right and continue to a junction. Turn left on the road leading to the park's merry-go-round. Park in the lower lot below the merry-go-round.

THE HIKE: Walk up the short asphalt road. Pass a trail on the left (this hike's return route) and a second trail on the left (Fern Canyon Nature Trail) and continue just a little farther to a three-way junction.

Bear left on unsigned Fern Canyon Trail and ascend the wide path into the brushy hills. Clouds of ceanothus accent sandstone cliffs. Enjoy clear-day views of the San Gabriel Mountains.

A mile from the trailhead, reach 5-Points, a five-way trail junction on a ridgeline. Two trails to the right head west toward Vista Valle Drive, while the engaging Coolidge Trail is the return route for this hike. Take the left-most trail, Upper Beacon Trail, and ascend a short distance along a brushy ridge to the top of Beacon Hill.

Imagine how Los Angeles must have looked to the airplane passenger in 1920: No freeways, no dramatic skyline. Not much there, there, then.

Today's clear-day vistas include downtown, Elysian Park, Silverlake Reservoir, freeways and freightyards, and the big bold "G" etched into the hill above Glendale. And the Los Angeles River, looking better with each passing year, as conservationists restore the cement-channeled waterway to something like its natural state, something like the pilots of old saw when they swooped in for a landing at Grand Central Airport.

Retrace your steps back to the 5-Points and stay left. Follow unsigned Coolidge Trail on a pleasant 1-mile descent south then east around Beacon Hill's south slope. Stay left at a fork and continue along unsigned Lower Beacon Trail, which parallels Griffith Park Drive along the east slope of Beacon Hill. In company with the din of the Golden State Freeway, the path trends west, and descends back to the trailhead.

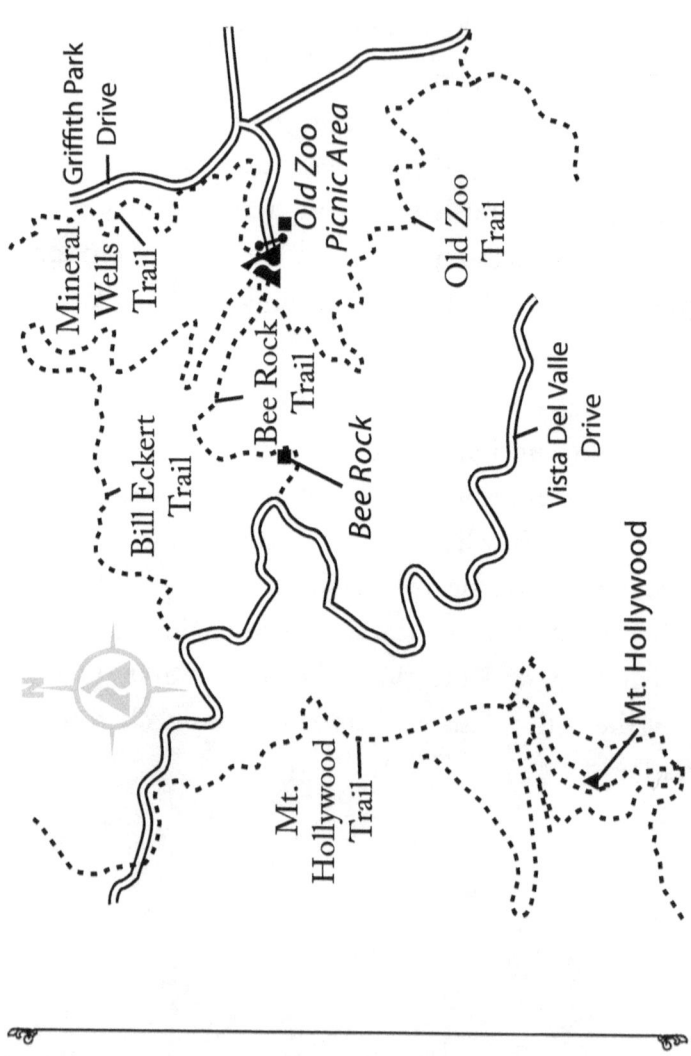

MT. HOLLYWOOD FROM OLD ZOO

BILL ECKERT, MT. HOLLYWOOD TRAILS

Old Zoo walkabout is 0.5 mile; From Old Zoo Picnic Area to Mt. Hollywood is 4.5 miles round trip with 1,000 foot elevation gain

One of the oddest sights-to-see in L.A. (and certainly the weirdest in Griffith Park) is the Old Zoo. The (old) Griffith Park Zoo opened in 1912 on the former site of Griffith J. Griffith's ostrich ranch and was significantly enlarged in the 1930s by construction crews from the Works Progress Administration.

The cave-like enclosures with iron bars were standard for zoos of that era, but as the years passed, the facilities were criticized for their ugliness and their prison-like confinement of the animals. The old zoo was closed in 1966 when the new Los Angeles Zoo was built two miles away.

Take a short hike around the Old Zoo and you'll discover the still-standing animal enclosures, lots of photo ops, and surely the strangest picnic area around.

One of my favorite routes to Mt. Hollywood starts from the site of the Old L.A. Zoo. It's officially labeled Bill Eckert Trail on park maps, though you won't find any such signage at the trailhead. Chief gardener for Ferndell during the 1950s, Eckert was a park ranger who shared his considerable enthusiasm and expertise on Griffith's flora and fascinating history.

DIRECTIONS: From Los Feliz Boulevard, head north on Crystal Springs Drive 1.5 miles to Griffith Park Drive. Turn left, travel 0.25 mile, and turn left into Old Zoo Picnic Area, then go 0.2 mile to parking on the left.

THE HIKE: Walk up the closed road and onto the fire road for 0.2 mile to a three-way junction. Make a hard right on Mineral Wells Trail and very shortly junction a second dirt road. This is Bill Eckert Trail; head left and start a vigorous ascent north. You got to love those views of Bee Rock and a strategically placed bench at a switchback offers metro vistas.

Pass two water towers on your right and the path curves west. When you reach the 1,000-foot elevation mark or so, enjoy great aerial views of Glendale, Burbank and beyond. Northern vistas of the Verdugo Mountains and San Gabriel Mountains are particularly good.

About 1.75 mile from the trailhead, the path ends at paved Vista Del Valle Drive (long ago closed to vehicle traffic). Turn right and walk 200 yards up to a junction with a dirt fire road on your left. Head uphill on this wide road, staying left at a trail split and ascending across the slopes of Mt. Bell and along a ridge to join Mt. Hollywood Trail.

Continue straight at a junction to the summit, picnic tables and vista point. Clear day or clear night, the views from Mt. Hollywood are always great: to the HOLLYWOOD Sign atop Mt. Lee to the west, Griffith Observatory below to the south, and a whole lot of metropolis at your feet.

Hike into the weird: Griffith Park's Old Zoo.

BEE ROCK

Fern Canyon, Old Zoo, Bee Rock Trails

To Bee Rock is 2.4 miles round trip with 150-foot elevation gain

Long a Griffith Park landmark, Bee Rock (1,056 feet), located on the western end of Griffith Park, offers great vistas of the San Fernando Valley, Verdugo Mountains and San Gabriel Mountains. On particularly clear days, eastern panoramas can take in Southland highpoint, Mt. San Gorgonio.

The beehive-shaped rock is a massive outcropping of sandstone. While such dramatic sedimentary formations are typical of what hikers encounter in Topanga State Park and in the middle of the Santa Monica Mountains, it's all the more dramatic here thrusting up from the hills overlooking the metropolis.

In 1903, a half-mile dirt road was constructed from Crystal Springs to the narrow canyon at the base of Bee Rock and the landmark has been popular with hikers ever since. Griffith J. Griffith was known to lead his fellow City of Los Angeles Parks Commissioners up to Bee Rock to survey the scene.

Enjoy this classic walk in the park and, on the return trip, wander over and visit the site of the Old Zoo. The (old) Griffith Park Zoo (1912-1966) still stands—too-small metal cages and all—and is a truly weird, must-see attraction.

Take a walking tour past the cramped enclosures and give thanks that treatment of zoo animals is better these days. You'll find great photo ops, and even a picnic area.

DIRECTIONS: Southbound on the Golden State Freeway (I-5), exit on Los Feliz Boulevard, turn left and cross the freeway. Turn right on Crystal Springs Drive, proceed 1.3 miles to an intersection. Turn left toward the merry-go-round parking lot. Ahead, this road is barricaded and you turn right into a large parking lot. Park close to the lot entrance. Northbound on the I-5, exit on Los Feliz, turn right, then another immediate right on Crystal Springs Drive.

THE HIKE: Walk up the paved road past the vehicle barrier. After passing a junction with Fern Canyon Nature Trail on your left, continue another 150 feet to a dirt road on the left. Leave the paved road for the dirt one (Fern Canyon Trail). Continue about 0.1 mile and, as the trail curves left, it meets Old Zoo Trail (a dirt road); bear right on this trail.

After a bit of ascent, observe Bee Rock, looming high above you.

Old Zoo Trail leads north then west through Spring Canyon and on the slopes above the old zoo. Across a seasonal creek, the trail angles northeast to a four-way junction about 0.75 from the trailhead. Mineral Wells Trail is straight ahead. Bear left on Bee Rock Trail (a dirt road).

The trail ascends 0.25 mile then continues as a narrow path, curving northwest and southeast, then switchbacking south toward Bee Rock. (Stick to the main trail, and avoid narrower and steeper use trails). Follow the path to the top of Bee Rock.

Enjoy those vistas despite the intrusive fence then head back the way you came. At the junction with Old Zoo Trail, continue instead on Bee Rock Trail and descend to the old zoo grounds. Wander around the too-tiny cages and long-abandoned enclosures, then join a path a bit lower than, and parallel to, Old Zoo Trail, leading back to Fern Canyon Trail and the trailhead.

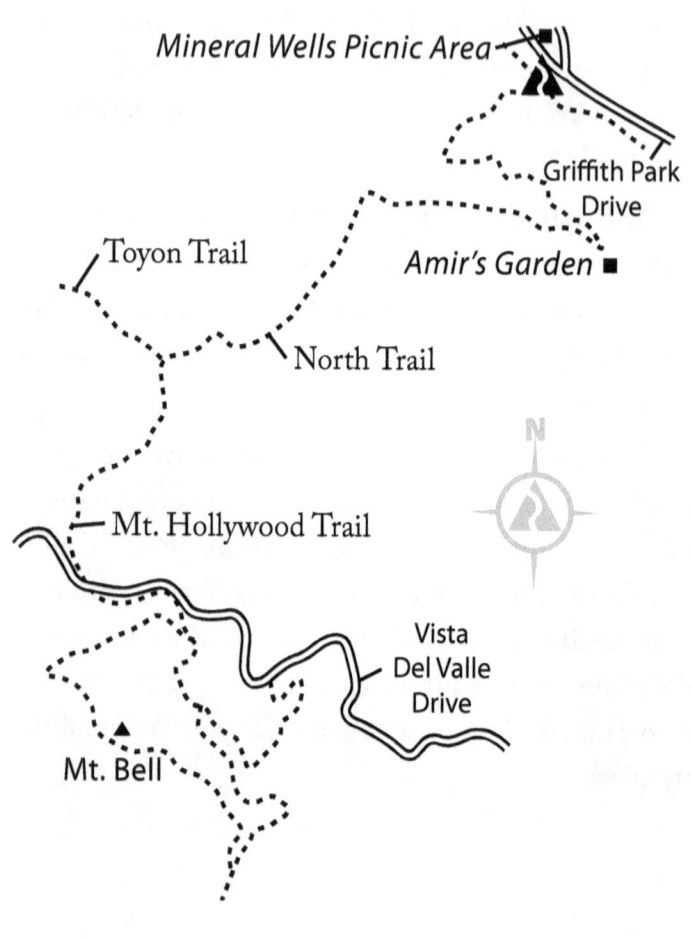

Amir's Garden & Mt. Bell
North, Mt. Hollywood Trails

From Mineral Wells Picnic Area to Amir's Garden is 1 mile round trip with 250-foot elevation gain; to Mt. Bell is 3.4 miles round trip with 800-foot gain

"My secrets to a healthy and happy life..." Amir Dialameh revealed to me one day as he tended his garden in the aerie heights of Griffith Park. "Being out in nature at least five days a week, staying away from doctors and lawyers, and hiking, lots of hiking."

The Iranian immigrant began fashioning his namesake two-acre oasis in 1971 following a severe fire that ravaged the brushy slopes above the Mineral Wells Picnic Area.

Dialameh hiked in the park and worked his garden nearly every single day. He passed away in 2003.

His slogan was "In the land of the free, plant a tree." Thankfully the garden did not burn in the great 2007 fire. Today, inspired by his example, volunteers tend Amir's Garden.

Amir's Garden is an easy goal for anyone desiring a quick escape from city life. Extend this hike to Mt. Bell (1,582 feet), located close to the center of Griffith Park. Views are great, with a particularly keen perspective due west at Mt. Lee and the HOLLYWOOD Sign.

DIRECTIONS: From the south side of the park on Los Feliz Boulevard, turn north on Griffith Park Drive and follow it just past Harding Golf Course clubhouse and driving range to Mineral Wells Picnic Area. Park in the picnic area and look for a three-way trail junction at the extreme lower end of the picnic ground, close to where the road splits to go around the picnic area.

THE HIKE: At the unsigned junction of three bridle trails, join the middle trail and ascend moderately to steeply a half-mile to Amir's Garden. Leave behind (some of) the din of the freeways and find an eclectic collection of pine and pepper trees, asparagus fern and spider plant, as well as a host of succulents.

Garden Tour complete, rejoin North Trail and ascend along a ridge above the Griffith Park Boys Camp. About 0.5 mile from Amir's Garden, reach a T-junction near a water tank. The right fork leads toward Toyon Canyon, a landscaped and terraced former dumpsite. Efforts to rehabilitate the canyon have been considerable; however, let's just say it does not remind one of Amir's Garden.

Stay left and go around the water tank and in about 250 feet pass a junction with Toyon Trail, a westbound footpath. Stick with the fire road (Mt. Hollywood Trail) on a southbound ascent to Vista Del Valle Drive. Follow the paved road (long closed to vehicles) 100 feet to the left and rejoin the trail on the right. The path parallels the road, offers fine "valle" vistas and reaches a trail fork 1.5 miles out. Bear right across the north shoulder of Mt. Bell. The trail splits again with the right fork extending to Mt. Hollywood Drive and the left heading for the south side of Mt. Bell. Look for a narrow summit trail that leads to the top.

"In the land of the free, plant a tree," declared Amir Dialameh, who tended his namesake garden for three decades.

Western Heritage

Skyline, Rattlesnake, Oak Canyon, Mineral Wells, Crystal Springs Trails

From Museum of the American West to Travel Town is 6 miles round trip with 300-foot elevation gain

Giddy-up! Griffith Park, with its brushy hills and dusty trails, has long been a popular locale for filming Westerns, so it seems fitting that the Museum of the American West (formerly Autry Museum of Western Heritage) is located here. The museum's displays of cowboy movie lore and other engaging exhibitions of the "real" West and the West of the imagination are top-notch. The museum also offers movie screenings, lectures, performances and art exhibits.

From the museum, take a hike to Travel Town, a collection of locomotives and engines, cars and trucks that tell the story of transportation in Southern California. Picnic en route or lunch at the museum's café.

DIRECTIONS: From the Golden State Freeway (5) or Ventura Freeway (134) exit on Zoo Drive and follow signs to the Los Angeles Zoo. Park opposite the zoo in the lot for the Museum of the American West.

THE HIKE: Walk across the lawn on the south side of the museum toward the freeway to a small corral and bear left (north) on the bridle trail. In 0.25 mile, pass through a tunnel under the southbound on-ramp then curve westward around the zoo parking lot. Look westward for a path that leads through two more pedestrian/equestrian underpasses to meet unsigned Skyline Trail about 0.5 mile from the start.

Ascend aggressive switchbacks west along the zoo boundary and get great views east of Glendale and Pasadena and north to the Walt Disney, Dreamworks and KABC studio complexes. Skyline Trail hikers see—and smell—Toyon Canyon, a former dumpsite in re-hab and an odorous composting facility nearby.

A mile's hike on the Skyline leads to Condor Trail, which branches left, and a half mile more to a junction with a welcome drinking fountain. (Skyline Trail continues west to Travel Town while an unnamed trail descends south to Griffith Park Drive.) Descend right (north) on steep Rattlesnake Trail 0.5 mile to Zoo Drive and L.A. Live Steamers, a scale-model railroad with rides (open Sundays).

Take "Main" Trail alongside the freeway 0.5 mile west or simply walk across the picnic area and alongside Zoo Drive to Travel Town. After stepping back into SoCal's transportation history, step across Griffith Park Drive and hike south on Oak Canyon Trail. The woodsy trail parallels the Drive, in 0.75 mile passes a junction with Mt. Hollywood Drive/Toyon Trail, and continues as Mineral Wells Trail 0.25 mile to Mineral Wells Picnic Area. Hike another 0.25 mile to a junction with the trail to Amir's Garden.

Another rolling mile on Mineral Wells Trail leads to Old Zoo Picnic Area and Park Center Picnic Area; improvise a route through the picnic area and cross Griffith Park Drive to Crystal Springs Drive and Crystal Springs Trail. Follow this path north alongside the golf courses. A bit more than a mile of level walking returns you to the museum and trailhead.

Griffith Park can still seem like the Wild West, coyotes and all.

BRONSON CAVE

BRONSON CAVE TRAIL

From Canyon Drive to Bronson Cave is 0.6 mile round trip with 50-foot elevation gain

"To the Bat Cave, Robin!" With that cry, Batman and Robin of television fame hopped into the Batmobile and sped off to their hideaway. The dynamic duo's underground lair was not, as you might guess, a movie set built on a studio back lot, but a real cave in the southwest corner of Griffith Park.

Batman (1966-68) was not the only television show to make use of the area known as the Bronson Caves. TV westerns from *Gunsmoke* to *Bonanza* to *Rawhide* used the caves as a hide-out for desperadoes. *Star Trek*, *Mission Impossible*, and many more shows filmed here.

The rock quarry operation that created the cave closed at the dawn of sound pictures and the location has been a popular with filmmakers ever since. My favorite classic films with Bronson Cave scenes include *I am a Fugitive from the Chain Gang* (1932) and *Invasion of the Body Snatchers* (1956). Many a low budget production filmed here, including *Teenagers from Outer Space* (1956), *They Saved Hitler's Brain* (1963) and *Vampire Boulevard* (2004).

Long before moviemakers discovered the caves, the rocky walls of the canyon were quarried by the Los Angeles Stone Company and used to form the rail-bed for the Pacific Electric Transit System. Excavation of crushed rock from Brush Canyon Quarry as it was known began in 1903 by the Union Quarry Company and continued until 1929. The crushed rock was used to construct streets in greater Los Angeles, including such major thoroughfares as Sunset and Wilshire boulevards.

In later years the cave and canyon became more commonly known at the Bronson Cave and Bronson Canyon after nearby Bronson Avenue. As the story goes, actor Charles Dennis Buchinsky dropped his Eastern European sounding name during the House Un-American Activities Committee (HUAC) proceedings of the 1950s and adopted the name "Bronson" from the name of the Paramount Studios Gate, avenue and canyon.

Through the magic of Hollywood, filmmakers have made the caves seem like they're located in the remote wilderness and with more movie magic have made the small cave seem like a large cavern.

The cave is actually a short tunnel and if shot head-on with by a cinematographer with a movie camera (or a hiker with a smart phone) the rear opening of the cave is easily visible. Therefore the cave entrance needs to be shot at an angle.

This is a great little walk for kids and out-of-town guests.

THE HIKE: Begin on Canyon Drive. At the top of Canyon Drive, you'll spot the trail and trailhead information display for Brush Canyon Trail, which leads to the HOLLYWOOD Sign. Depending on where you park, you'll need to backtrack along Canyon Drive down to a dirt road on the right (as you look up the road).

Follow the dirt road southeast 0.25 mile to reach a junction and angle left to the bowl-shaped quarry site. And there it is: Bronson Cave, which at first glance looks like a drive-through tunnel in a 100-foot high rock wall.

Check out the main passage where the Batmobile was garaged and two smaller passageways of duck-and-crawl size. No flashlight required.

Return the way you came with the added treat of a view of the HOLLYWOOD Sign.

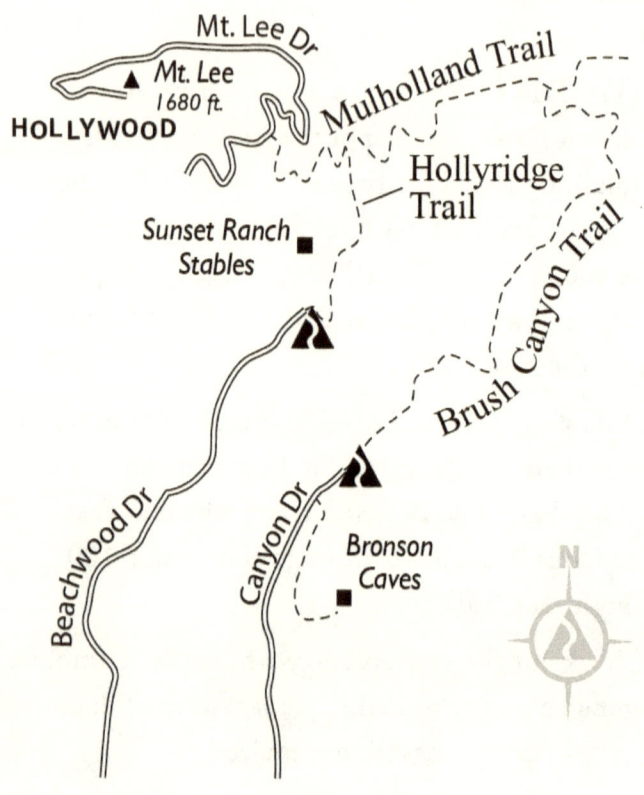

TheTrailmaster.com

Hollywood Sign from Brush Canyon

Brush Canyon, Mulholland, Mt. Lee Trails

From Canyon Drive to HOLLYWOOD Sign is 6.4 miles round trip with 1,100-foot elevation gain

Located in the southeast area of the Griffith Park, Brush Canyon is less developed and less crowded than other areas of the park. Cloaked in chaparral, Brush Canyon definitely lives up to its name. Apparently its brushy nature was not a secret; "Brush Canyon" was on the map in the early years of the 20th century—even before the park was established.

But brush isn't the only flora in the Brush Canyon. Oak and sycamore thrive in the bottom of the canyon.

Along with offering a convenient trailhead for a hike to the HOLLYWOOD Sign, Brush Canyon is an ideal place to start for a sojourn to other nearby summits—particularly the three noteworthy peaks that rise above the ridges of the canyon: Mt. Bell, Mt. Chapel and Mt. Hollywood.

Due to the closure of the Hollyridge Trail, Canyon Drive trailhead has become a favorite trailhead for a hike to the HOLLYWOOD Sign. Expect lots of company on the trail from SoCal hikers and visitors from across the US and around the world.

DIRECTIONS: From Franklin Avenue, on the southern boundary of Griffith Park, turn north on Bronson Avenue or Canyon Drive (the streets soon join and continue as Canyon). Follow Canyon Drive a winding mile through the hills into Griffith Park. Park alongside the road or in a lot near a picnic area or in a small parking lot by the trailhead at road's end. Note: Park authorities *close* the road at sunset.

THE HIKE: Those heading directly for the Bronson Caves will locate the trailhead on the right

Bronson Cave, starring in major motion pictures and cult favorites.

(east) side of Canyon Drive. Join a fire road and hike south a short distance to the caves.

Walk past an info board with a large park map and join the fire road (Brush Canyon Trail). The trail passes handsome sycamores that line the canyon bottom but once the trail begins climbing northeast it leaves the trees behind and Brush Canyon lives up to its name. Chaparral flora frame views of the HOLLYWOOD Sign and Mt. Hollywood.

After 1.25 miles and a stiff 600-foot gain, reach an overlook (great views of metro LA) and soon thereafter a signed junction with Mulholland Trail, a wide dirt road. Go left (west) on a more level course, pass a junction with Hollyridge Trail (that leads to the closed Beachwood Drive trailhead). Keep right, and wind west to meet Mt. Lee Drive, 2.2 miles from the trailhead.

A 0.4-mile descent on Mt. Lee Drive leads to Hollywood Sign View (great views indeed and photo ops galore from this overlook; see hike description from Innsdale Drive). Ascend the steep paved road about 1 mile to the summit and a view of DOOWYLLOH, those giant white capital letters from above and behind the sign.

A locked gate prevents hikers from reaching the top of Mt. Lee. But do enjoy the views from about 100 feet above the HOLLYWOOD Sign. Resist the urge to climb over the fence in order to have your picture taken next to the sign; it's strictly illegal.

Choose among a half-dozen fun hikes to the HOLLYWOOD Sign.

EVERY TRAIL TELLS A STORY.

II
Hollywood Hills

HIKE ON.

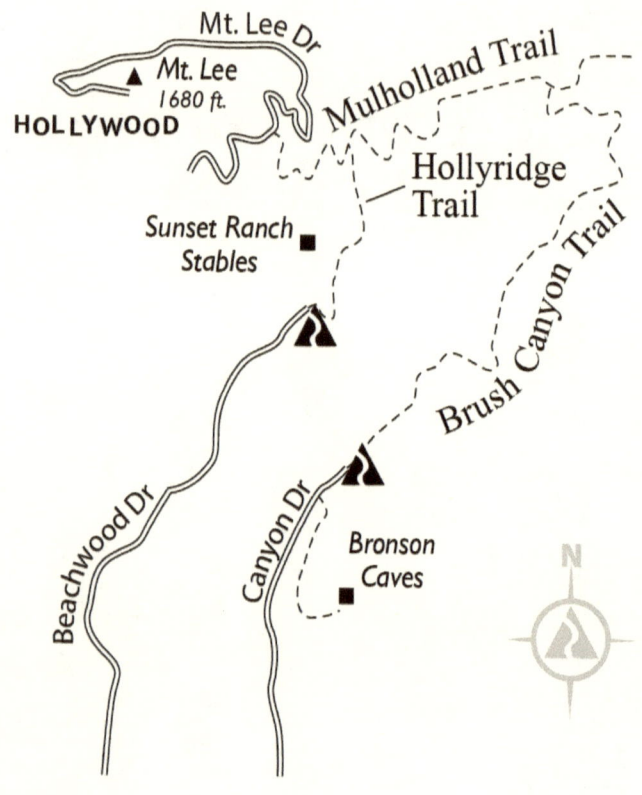

Hollywood Sign from Beachwood Drive

Hollyridge, Mulholland, Mt. Lee Trails

From Beachwood Drive to Hollywood Sign is 3 miles round trip with 500-foot elevation gain

Hollyridge Trail, once the most popular path to the HOLLYWOOD Sign is the subject of a multi-party trailhead access dispute involving Sunset Stables, City Parks, Friends of Griffith Park, homeowner groups and scores of hikers. At this writing, Hollyridge Trail is closed.

To make sure everyone knew about the new Beachwood Canyon real estate development, the developers, ordered a huge wooden sign built atop Mt. Lee. Back in the early 1920s, it read HOLLYWOODLAND.

Never kept in the best repair, letters—particularly the "H"—frequently blew down. In 1923, a depressed actress leaped from the sign. During a 1949 gale, the sign lost its LAND. In 1978, the HOLLYWOOD sign was restored to its former glory.

You can hike close to the top of the large (50 feet high, 450 feet long) sign, but not all the way to it because the iconic landmark is fenced-off. Besides the sign, 1,640-foot Mt. Lee has another claim to fame: L.A.'s first television signals were broadcast from the peak in the 1940s.

This hike, an L.A. classic, offers a visit to the world-renowned HOLLYWOOD Sign, as well as views along the way of Burbank, the San Fernando Valley and, of course, Hollywood.

DIRECTIONS: In Hollywood, from its intersection with Franklin Avenue, head north on Beachwood Drive and ascend 1.7 miles to the end of the public road. Park along Beachwood Monday through Friday, but note that there is NO parking on Saturday and Sunday. (Trailhead access subject to change.)

THE HIKE: Hollyridge Trail heads up a small hill to almost instant vistas: the HOLLYWOOD Sign in postcard view and a little farther along, looking very sci-fi from this angle, the dome of the Griffith Observatory. Hike northeast along the ridge above the Sunset Stables.

A half-mile out, reach an unsigned junction with Mulholland Trail. The right branch leads into Griffith Park to intersect Mt. Hollywood Drive and a trail to Mt. Hollywood. Take the left fork of the fire road, wind west 0.3 mile to an intersection with Mt. Lee Drive, and turn right. Ascend the paved road and gain excellent clear- day views of Forest Lawn, downtown Burbank, and the Valley beyond.

(Just short of the summit, as the road makes a sharp left bend, look for a signed junction with a trail leading westward to Cahuenga Peak; this could be a fun add-on to the hike to the sign.)

Continue on the road. A locked gate prevents hikers from reaching the top of Mt. Lee. But do enjoy the metropolitan views, perhaps in the company from visitors from around the world, from above the HOLLYWOOD Sign.

Hollyridge Trail: Classic pathway closed for now, but not forgotten.

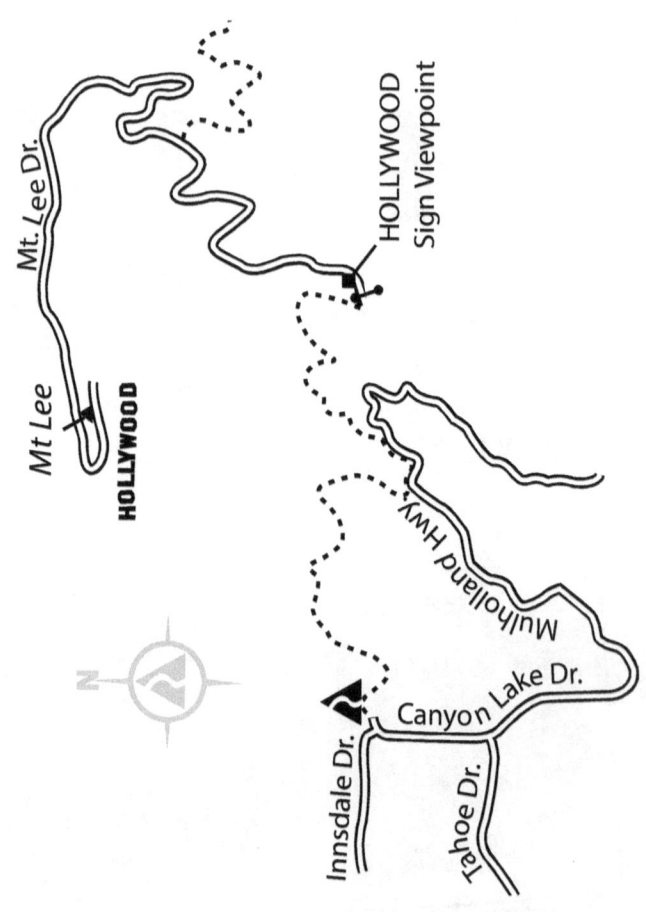

Hollywood Sign from Innsdale Drive

Innsdale Trail, Mt. Lee Road

From Innsdale Drive to Hollywood Sign Viewpoint is 2 miles round trip with 200-foot elevation gain; to HOLLYWOOD Sign is 4.6 miles round trip with 700-foot gain

This hike does not save the best for last. Great views of the HOLLYWOOD Sign are yours from the beginning of the hike, which makes it highly appealing to the many visitors from across the nation and around the world looking for the easiest way to get photo ops.

A combination of winding streets and dirt fire roads lead a short mile to Hollywood Sign Viewpoint, aka Selfie Heaven. Frame your photos with the flora en route: cactus, California holly, palm trees, bougainvillea and bamboo.

Please be on your best hiker behavior: The classic Hollyridge Trail was closed under pressure from private property owners; no guarantee the route from Innsdale Drive will always be open.

DIRECTIONS: From northbound Highway 101, exit on Barham Drive and drive north 0.3 mile to Lake Hollywood Drive. Turn right and follow the winding road, passing a junction with Wonder View Drive, then Lake Hollywood Reservoir. After 1.5 miles, turn left on Tahoe Drive and continue 0.25 mile to Canyon Lake Drive. Find curbside parking where you can, and the trailhead located 0.1 mile at the end of Canyon Lake Drive at Innsdale Drive.

THE HIKE: Walk up the wide dirt road (Innsdale Trail for lack of a better name) and…wow, there it is, the HOLLYWOOD Sign. Curve around a bend and just 0.25-mile out, you'll find yourself directly below the letters. Wow!

The fire road angles right toward houses and at the 0.5-mile mark, squeeze past a driveway and reach a residential street (Mulholland). Turn left, and make another left at the first junction. March past a thicket of signs, ascend past a last house to reach a dirt road, and wind across a hillside above the HollywoodLand neighborhood.

A short mile from the trailhead, the dirt trail ends at a teal-colored gate. Ascend steps to a paved road located at the crest of Deronda Drive to meet Mt. Lee Drive and a junction. Walk 100 yards up the paved service road (toward a water tank) to Hollywood Sign View. Join visitors from around the world, nearly all taking and posting photos.

Back to business and the route to the Hollywood Sign: 1.3 more miles up paved Mt. Leet Drive. As you ascend get views of Griffith Observatory and Mt. Hollywood to the east, and downtown L.A. to the southeast and, in 0.3 mile, meet a dirt fire road (Mulholland Trail) that leads toward Brush Canyon (see hike description). Keep left on the paved road for the final mile, and get more views: the Verdugo Mountains, San Gabriel Mountains and downtown Burbank.

Just short of the summit, look right and note the signed junction with steep Aileen Getty Ridge Trail that leads to Cahuenga Peak. (A great add-on to this hike!) Minutes later, pass along the chain link fence separating the road from the sign, and reach a vista point above the 'H' in the HOLLYWOOD Sign. Enjoy!

Be sure to stop at Hollywood Sign Overlook, aka Selfie Heaven.

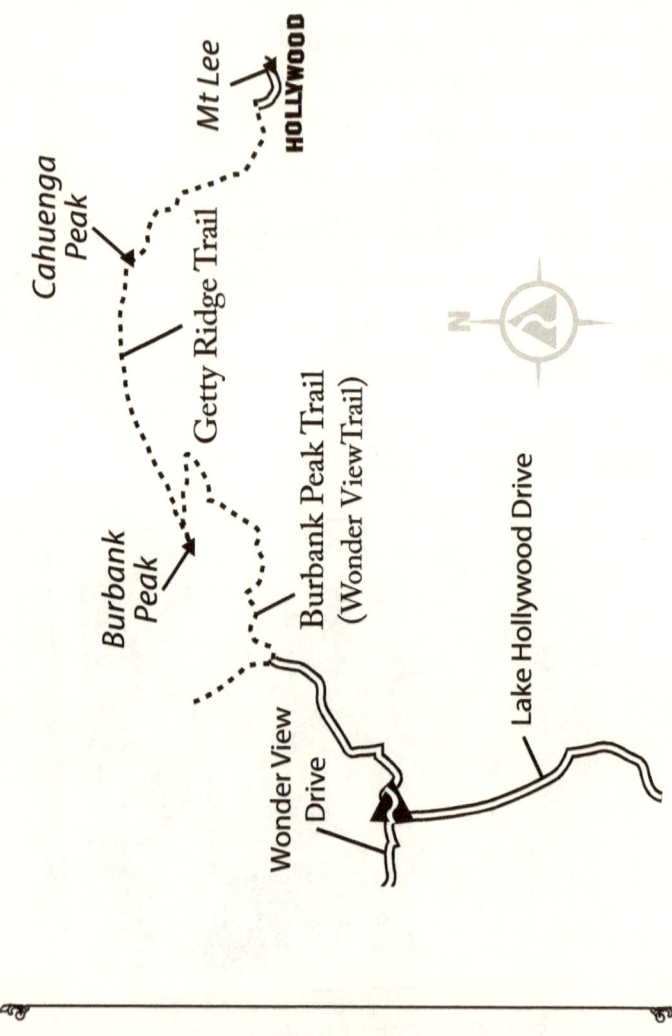

Hollywood Sign from Wonderview Drive

Burbank Peak, Getty Ridge, Mt. Lee Trails

From Wonder View Drive to Cahuenga Peak is 2.4 miles round trip with 900-foot elevation gain; to Mt Lee is 3.2 miles round trip

Wonder View Trail leads to the 1,820-foot summit of Cahuenga Peak, high point of the Hollywood Hills. The narrow and steep path (a true hiker's route) continues to nearby Mt. Lee, which hosts the famed HOLLYWOOD Sign.

In 2010, hikers and movie fans from across the nation and around the world were delighted to learn that creative conservation efforts, combined with fundraising from private and public sectors, succeeded in purchasing the peak and adding it to Griffith Park.

When the developers announced plans to subdivide the peak into luxury estates, local conservationists, film fans, and celebs rallied to "Save the Peak." Some

$12 million was raised to purchase the 138-acre site. Hollywood notables, including Steven Spielberg and Tom Hanks, plus the Tiffany & Company Foundation, Hugh Hefner and Aileen Getty contributed serious cash, as did state and local agencies.

As the story goes, Cahuenga, which names a pass, a peak and nowadays a boulevard was once a native Shoshone village located on the banks of the Los Angeles River near present-day Universal City. The peak is the 12th highest in the Hollywood Hills/Santa Monica Mountains.

DIRECTIONS: From Highway 101 in North Hollywood, exit on Barham Boulevard and head north 0.3 mile. Turn right on Lake Hollywood Drive and continue 0.5 mile to intersect Wonder View Drive (no street parking). Park alongside Lake Hollywood Drive.

THE HIKE: Walk 0.25 mile up paved Wonder View Drive to its end. Hike past a yellow vehicle gate on dirt road 300 feet to unsigned Burbank Peak Trail (formerly Wonder View Trail) on your right. Begin a steep eastward ascent east, zigzagging up the south slope of Cahuenga Peak. Enjoy wonderful views of Mt. Lee with its forest of antennae, Griffith Observatory, Mt. Hollywood and downtown L.A.

After a quite aggressive 0.8-mile climb the rough trail gains a ridgeline and splits: the signed right fork leads to Cahuenga Peak and a short pathway deposits. A short side trail leads left to a lone pine tree and the top of Burbank Peak (1,690 feet). Pause to read the summit logbook stashed below the Wisdom Tree; hikers have been know to get very creative with their philosophizing in this book. Clear-day panoramic views are terrific—particularly angles on the San Fernando Valley and San Gabriel Mountains.

Join signed Aileen Getty Ridge Trail and hike east along a ridgeline 0.3 mile to the summit of Cahuenga Peak. The path then drops to a saddle between Cahuenga Peak and Mt. Lee (1,680 feet) and ends at Mount Lee Road. Turn right and walk up the paved road to the viewpoint above the HOLLYWOOD Sign.

Add your own wisdom to the hiker register at the Wisdom Tree.

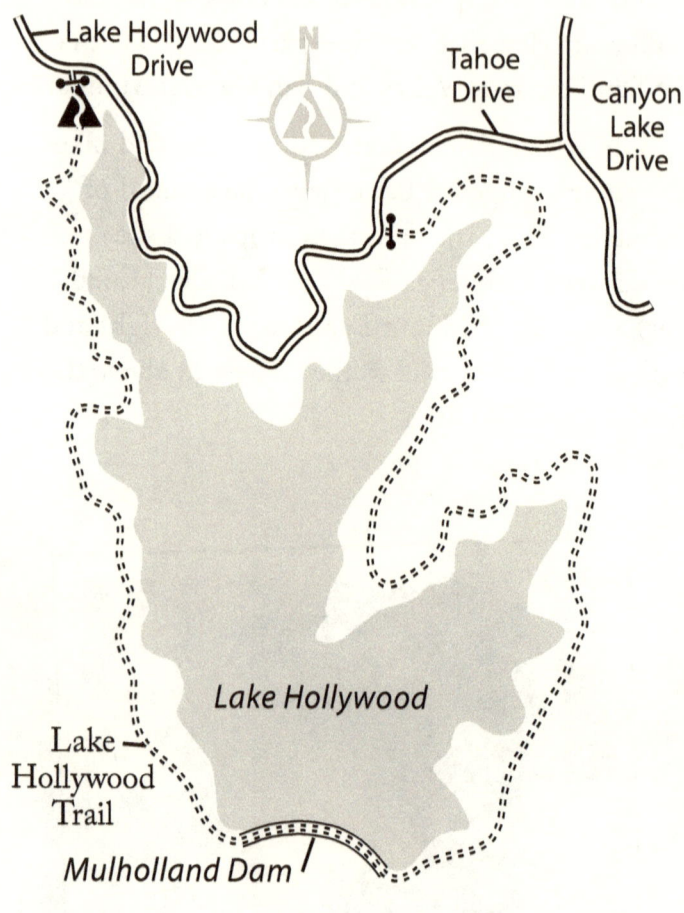

Hollywood Reservoir
Lake Hollywood Trail

From North Gate to Mulholland Dam is 2 miles round trip; 4-mile loop on adjacent streets

Nestled in the Hollywood Hills, this lovely lake is one of the quietest and most secluded bodies of water in the city. The pathway around the lake, an asphalt service road (closed to vehicles), is a favorite exercise circuit for locals and stressed-out film industry folks.

As a locale, Lake Hollywood has a high profile and attracts tourist traffic; not much, though, in comparison to the nearby HOLLYWOOD Sign. It's also a walk everybody in L.A. likes to say they've done once.

It's been the backdrop for many movies, contemporary and classic. Scenes in "Chinatown," the 1974 movie that showed the slimy side of Los Angeles water and power struggles, were shot around the lake. In another 1974 film, "Earthquake," the reservoir dam collapsed and flooded the city below.

Compared to some of the city's other, more utilitarian-looking reservoirs, Hollywood gets an "A" for Aesthetics. It was built in 1925 by city water commissioner William Mulholland as part of the city's gigantic waterworks program designed to secure, ship, and store water for the rapidly expanding population of Los Angeles. The reservoir's 2.5 billion gallons of water are held by Mulholland Dam; the walk across it and great views are highlights of this excursion.

Less concerned with aesthetics than with evaporation, possible sabotage and water quality laws, the Los Angeles Department of Water and Power once had plans to cover the lake; however, in response to neighborhood and citywide protests, two large underground storage were built instead on the north side of the reservoir.

Heads-up for hikers: 1) A chain-link fence and high vegetation preclude more than an occasional glimpse of the lake—until reaching the top of the dam. 2) Portions of the service road on the west side of the lake were closed by landslides in 2005 and restoration efforts have been going on for years; don't count on making a loop.

DIRECTIONS: From the Hollywood Freeway (101) in Los Angeles (Universal City area) exit on Barham Boulevard and head north 0.2 mile to Lake Hollywood Drive. Turn right and follow it 0.7 mile, winding east and south through a residential area. Park along the Drive near the gate to the reservoir. The path is open from 6:30 to 10 a.m. and 2 to 5 p.m. daily, and 6:30 a.m. to 7:30 p.m. weekends.

THE HIKE: The pine-shaded service road soon isolates you from the noise of the city; the effect is rather like that of moving through a green tunnel. Lake views are dramatic when you cross over to the south side of the reservoir via the top of Mulholland Dam. The view includes the HOLLYWOOD Sign, reflections on the lake above and the metropolis below.

Continue along the west side of the reservoir until reaching the limits of the repaired road; if passable, continue to the reservoir gate on Tahoe Drive. Walk 0.75 mile to Lake Hollywood Drive and the hike starting point.

Beauty and the peaks: Lake Hollywood and high points of Griffith Park

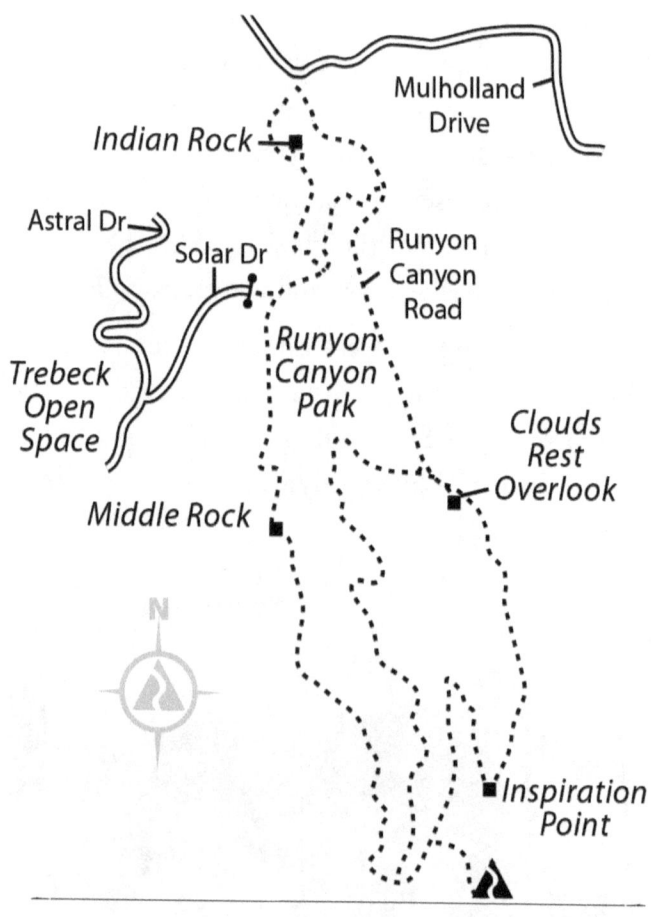

Runyon Canyon Park

Runyon Canyon Trail

2.7-mile loop with 700-foot elevation gain

No Man's Canyon was the earliest name given to the deep arroyo that nature sculpted in the Hollywood Hills. A century-and-a-half ago, it was the wild domain of birds and rabbits, coyotes and lizards.

Today Runyon Canyon is the most popular place in L.A. to hike. According to the Friends of Runyon Canyon, some 1.8 million people a year visit the canyon, with about 35,000 coming each week! The park was closed for repairs for four months in 2016 and reopened with more drinking fountains for people and pets and a repaving of the 137-acre park's main trail.

In 1867 Army Camel Corps officer "Greek George" Caralambo acquired the canyon. Coal magnate Carmen Runyon bought it in 1919 and built a hunting lodge and actor/singer John McCormick (hit movie, "Song of My Heart") purchased the canyon in 1929 and built a mansion called San Patrizio.

In 1942, wealthy arts patron Huntington Hartford bought the estate and renamed it "The Pines." Later owners tried to develop a subdivision of luxury homes. In 1984, the City of Los Angeles purchased Runyon Canyon and created a park.

Runyon Canyon has three trails, which connect and loop: paved main trail, the most gently sloping and easiest; the west trail, steepest and most challenging; the east trail, which leads to Inspiration Point. Every Runyon regular has a favorite route; for first-timers, I recommend a counterclockwise loop that allows several options.

DIRECTIONS: From the Hollywood Freeway in Hollywood, exit on Highland Avenue and head south past the Hollywood Bowl to Franklin Avenue. Turn west on Franklin and drive 0.3 mile to Fuller Avenue. Turn right and proceed a short distance to road's end at The Pines entrance gate to Runyon Park. Street parking is where you find it.

THE HIKE: Enter the park via the wrought iron gate, observe the wide lawn that hosts yoga classes, and soon reach a trail junction. A wide dirt road leads left, but continue straight on the main trail and 0.5 mile from the start reach Inspiration Point. Enjoy metro views and continue on a steeper ascent by wooden steps and trail along the park's east ridge 0.3 mile to Cloud's Rest, another vista point. Hike on and soon reach a junction. (Go left, descend to the canyon bottom and loop back to the trailhead to complete a 1.7 mile hike.)

Ascend 0.4 mile to meet a fire road. (To reach park high point Indian Rock (1,325 feet), head right, hike 0.2 mile toward the trailhead on Mulholland Drive, turn left and join a dirt trail that turns south, then take a side trail to the high point. Backtrack, to the junction with the west ridge trail and head south; this adds 0.5 mile to the hike.)

Turn left and soon pass the trail coming down from Indian Rock. Descend along the canyon's west side as the route narrows to a footpath. Enjoy views south of the metropolis but watch your step on the quick and steep drop to the Vista Street Gate. Head back to the center of the canyon and complete the loop.

Happy—and very popular—trails in Runyon Canyon.

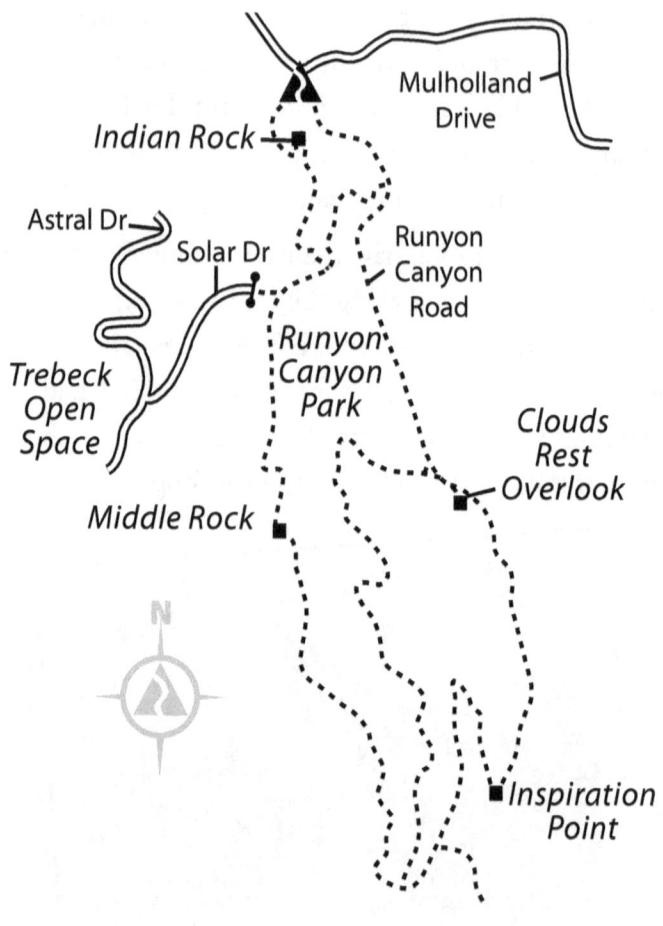

Runyon Canyon Park (North)

Runyon Canyon Trail

From Mulholland Drive, a 2.5 mile loop with 500-foot elevation gain

For convenience, most walkers, runners and hikers use the southern entrance to Runyon Canyon located close to Hollywood Boulevard. However, the 130-acre park extends to Mulholland Drive and offers two northern trailheads for access to the canyon's charms.

Don't expect solitude on a walk in the northern part of the park, but you'll definitely find fewer fellow travelers at the top of the canyon than at the bottom. The northern trailheads also give easy trail access to terrific metropolitan vistas. In fact the time-pressed hiker can make a bee-line for park highpoint Indian Rock and take in the city scene.

From the park's vista points, get good views of the rooftop pools of Hollywood hotels, the pagoda of Grauman's Chinese Theater, Hollywood Boulevard,

Sunset Strip, Capitol Records Building, Pacific Design Center, Century City, Wilshire high-rises, and much more. Look east to Griffith Observatory and the HOLLYWOOD Sign, southeast to downtown Los Angeles and southwest to Santa Monica Bay, Catalina Island and the wide blue Pacific.

DIRECTIONS: In Hollywood, exit the Hollywood Freeway (Highway 101) on Barham Boulevard, turn left on Cahuenga Boulevard and drive a half-mile. At Mulholland Drive make a right then an immediate left and wind 1.5 miles into the hills to trailhead parking on the left side of the road and a gated entry road to Runyon Canyon Park on the right. To reach the park's most obscure trailhead: From Hollywood Boulevard, head north on Nichols Canyon Road 1.5 miles to Astral Drive. Turn right and travel 0.2 mile to Solar Drive, and follow it briefly to its end at a gate on the west boundary of Runyon Canyon Park. Find limited curbside parking.

THE HIKE: From the trailhead, fork right to visit 1,320-foot Indian Rock, high point of Runyon Canyon Park. Enjoy the 360-degree vista from the summit—including the San Fernando Valley and points north. Continue on the trail to intersect the park's westernmost path.

If you take the left fork at the trailhead, you'll head out on the paved pathway that bends around Indian Rock and leads 0.2 mile to a junction. Bear right and head uphill, soon passing a short side trail leading to the park's Solar Drive entrance. About 0.4 mile of road-walking leads to the footpath network in Trebeck Open Space (see hike description).

Continuing south, the trail traverses the ridgeline between Runyon and Nichols canyons to 1,218-foot Middle Rock and more stellar panoramic views. Descend farther along the ridgeline trail to the canyon bottom, where the path bends south through a eucalyptus grove.

Easiest return is by way of the paved path ascending moderately along the west wall of Runyon Canyon. In about the middle of the park, the road bends east to meet Runyon Canyon Road. Clouds Rest Overlook (more great views!) is just south, while the return route is north, traveling the east side of the park back to the trailhead.

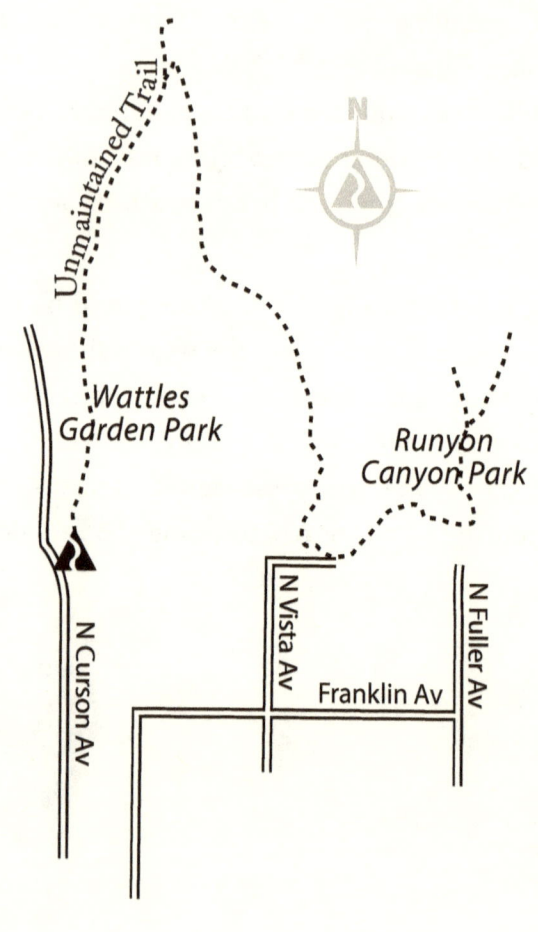

WATTLES GARDEN PARK

WATTLES GARDEN TRAIL

Garden Tour is 1 round trip; loop via Runyon Canyon is 3 miles round trip with 350-foot elevation gain

Located only a block from Hollywood Boulevard, Wattles Garden Park offers a bucolic retreat and an intriguing look back into the early history of Hollywood. Enjoy an easy one-mile walk and an altogether different sightseeing experience.

Or you can take a walk on the wild side. Experienced hikers and those in top condition can trek a steep and sketchy trail leading to Runyon Canyon Park and loop back via trails and city streets.

Prior to moving to Los Angeles, Gordon Wattles ran the streetcar company in Omaha, Nebraska. The wealthy tycoon commissioned prominent local architects Myron Hunt and Elmer Grey to design a magnificent Mission Revival-style mansion in 1907. The grounds featured a Spanish garden, Japanese garden, and Italian rose garden, and became one of Hollywood's first tourist attractions.

Today the 50 acre estate is administered by the Los Angeles Recreation and Parks Department and the mansion is open only to private, permitted events. Quite a place for a wedding! The urban hiker can explore the grounds and catch a clear-day views of the city, coast, and Catalina Island.

As for the trail leading from Wattles Garden Park to Runyon Canyon Park, it's narrow and very steep and not "a walk in the park," as the saying goes. Give yourself plenty of time to make the ascent. Once you make it to the ridgeline of Runyon Canyon, though, it's an all-downhill hike and return trip by city sidewalks to Wattles Garden Park.

DIRECTIONS: Wattles Garden Park entrance is located at 1824 North Curson Avenue, one block north of Hollywood Boulevard. Park wherever you can find a spot along Curson Avenue.

THE HIKE: Start the easy part of this adventure at the lower garden gates. Below lies Wattles Farm, a 4-acre community garden created in 1975 and one of the older community gardens in the city. Walk up the driveway to the porch of Wattles Mansion. What a place!

Return to Curson Avenue, head uphill, and re-enter Wattles Garden through the park's upper gate.

Wander the grounds, admire the Japanese Garden. Look for a right-forking dirt path and a granite staircase lined with short pillars that leads to a traditional Japanese shrine. This is the end of the easy walk.

Ask yourself: Do I really want to hike up *that* canyon? If so, begin hiking. Notice the right-forking short side trail that leads to…let's call it "Hippie Garden" leading to "OHM SPOT" and "This Wall built with Peace and Love."

The trail, marked occasionally by rock cairns, narrows and heads straight up without a single switchback. The good news is that while uneven, the foot is pretty good and the path is not brush-crowded.

Just when you begin to doubt you're ever going to reach the top, you might hear voices—from the many hikers in Runyon Canyon. When you intersect the park trail, go right, downhill and follow the main trail, part dirt/part paved to the bottom of the canyon.

Exit the park through either Fuller or Vista Gate and descend a block to Franklin. Turn right and walk a few blocks along Franklin to Sierra Bonita. Continue straight ahead through the back gate of Wattles Garden Park along the paved park road past the community gardens. Cross the mansion grounds back to the Curson Avenue.

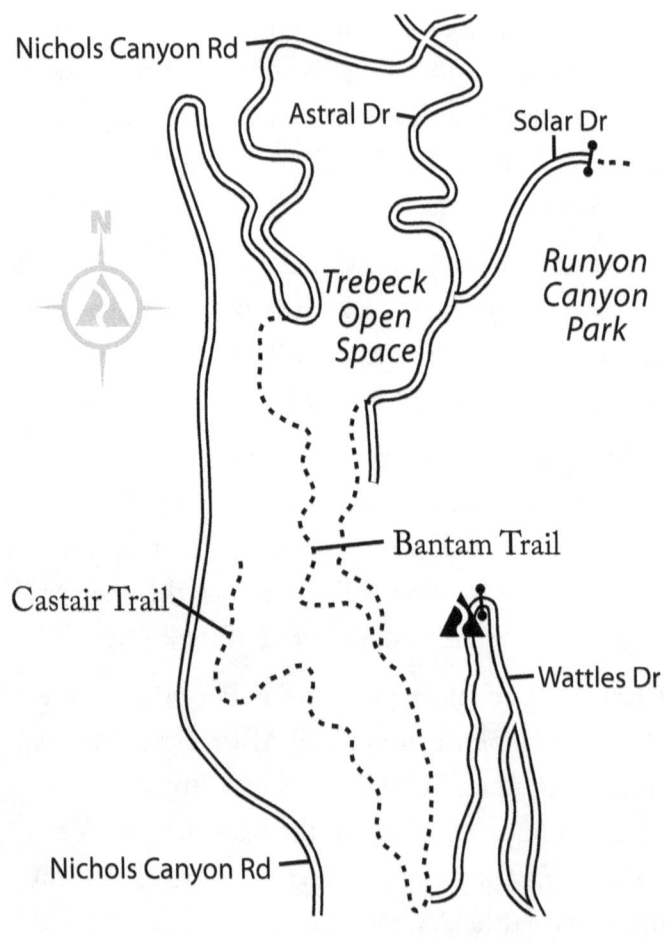

TREBECK OPEN SPACE

CASTAIR AND BANTAM TRAILS

From Wattles Drive to Overlooks is 2.5 miles round trip with 300-foot elevation gain

Alex Trebek, host of the popular game show "Jeopardy!" donated 62 acres of open land in the Hollywood Hills to the Santa Monica Mountains Conservancy in 1998. The much-needed parkland north of Hollywood Boulevard offers trails and fire roads for hikers, joggers and cyclists.

Trebek's terrain is similar to that of popular Runyon Canyon located just east and offers hikers the same great views. The biggest difference between the two is the amount of foot traffic, human and canine. Compared to popular Runyon Canyon, Trebek Open Space is lightly visited, almost undiscovered.

Trebeck's primary trails, Castair and Bantam, climb south-facing slopes and lead to overlooks. While Trebek Open Space is located adjacent to Runyon Canyon Park and Wattles Garden, no trail connects these public lands; however a little residential road-walking will take you from Trebek to Runyon.

DIRECTIONS: From Hollywood Boulevard, six blocks west of Fairfax, head north on Curson Avenue 0.5 mile to its end at a meeting with gated Wattles Drive. Park curbside near the top of Curson. (To access Trebek Open Space from its upper (northern) section, take Hollywood Boulevard to Nichols Canyon Road and drive north 1.3 miles.)

THE HIKE: From the pedestrian gate on Wattles Drive, walk south past modern manses to the beginning of a dirt road 0.2 mile from the trailhead. Walk 100 feet up the dirt road and look sharply right for a steep, sketchy, single-track trail heading up the hillside; this is the very rough start of Bantam Trail.

For now, continue straight ahead on Castair Trail, a mellow dirt road that soon bends north and travels along the east wall of Nichols Canyon. Artist David Hockney once lived in Nichols Canyon and painted "Nichols Canyon" in 1980. Reach an overlook and enjoy metropolitan views. Beyond the overlook, Castair Trail ends unceremoniously at fenced-off private property.

Retrace your steps a half mile to the aforementioned tentative beginning of Bantam Trail. Once you surmount the first 50 feet or so, Bantam Trail gets better. The path levels atop a hillock then ascends a chaparral-cloaked ridgeline to a vista point located about 250 feet below a trail junction.

From the junction, left-forking Bantam Trail travels the east wall of Nichols Canyon (above Castair Trail) and leads to a vista point with commanding views of the sprawling metropolis. A last length of Bantam Trail extends to a gate at Nichols Canyon Road.

Choose the right fork to make a ridgeline ascent. Look east over to the well-traveled trails in Runyon Canyon Park; to reach the park, continue to trail's end at Astral Drive. Ascend north on Astral Drive and bear right on Solar Drive, hoofing it to its end at a gated entrance to the park. Figure about 0.4 mile to reach the park's north boundary at Mulholland and more than a mile of hiking to the heart of the park and south entrance.

Even Beverly Hills has its wild side and hiking trails.

EVERY TRAIL TELLS A STORY.

III
Far Eastern Santa Monica Mountains

HIKE ON.

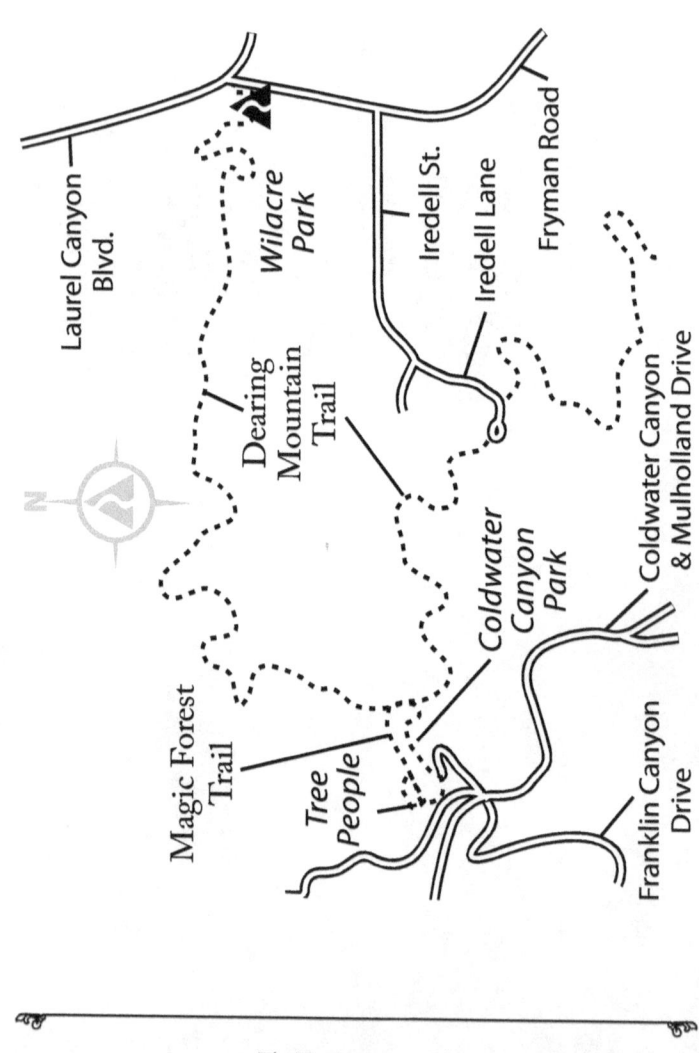

WILACRE PARK AND COLDWATER CANYON

Dearing Mountain Trail

From Wilacre Park to Coldwater Canyon Park is 2.7 miles round trip with 400-foot elevation gain

The wilds of Studio City offer the hiker several attractions: Wilacre Park (the former estate of silent movie cowboy Will Acres), great clear-day vistas of the San Fernando Valley, and Coldwater Canyon Park, longtime headquarters of TreePeople, an organization that has successfully promoted countless tree-planting projects in Los Angeles.

TreePeople Headquarters was once Fire Station 108, built by the Los Angeles Fire Department in 1923. During the years the firemen were in residence, eucalyptus, pine and many other kinds of nonnative trees were planted in the area.

You can learn about the trees by taking Magic Forest Nature Trail, which winds through the preserve. Scores of school kids take eco-tour field trips to Coldwater Canyon Park, "one of the 300 best reasons to stay in Los Angeles," according to Los Angeles Magazine.

Another alteration is the terracing of hillsides to create pads for the construction of homes. Building on steep slopes is, of course, prevalent in canyons all around Southern California, but in the Coldwater-Laurel Canyon area it has reached astonishing heights. The hiker looks up at some truly astonishing residences—homes on stilts, homes built stairstep-like down precipitous canyon walls, homes that seem certain to slide down to Ventura Boulevard after the first good rain.

Dearing Mountain Trail leads from Wilacre Park to Coldwater Canyon Park; with a half-mile walk on residential streets you can make this jaunt on a loop hike. (Also, see hike description to Fryman Canyon Overlook on Mulholland Drive.)

DIRECTIONS: From the Ventura Freeway (101) in Studio City, exit on Laurel Canyon Boulevard, drive south 1.5 miles to Fryman Canyon Road. Turn right and park in the lot; if it's full, look for street parking nearby. The unsigned trail begins at a yellow vehicle gate.

THE HIKE: Ascend the asphalt road past bay laurel and towering toyon, walnut trees and assorted planted pines. The road (onetime entry to Will Acres' property) retires to dirt just after passing the foundation ruins of his old house. The path offers terrific clear-day vistas of the San Fernando Valley, turns south, descends a bit and, at a wide spot in the road, 1.4 miles from the trailhead, intersects Coldwater Canyon Park's Magic Forest Trail.

Continue on Dearing Mountain Trail or, if you want a little break, detour right on the park's nature trail. Ascend one of the handsome stone staircases, built by the WPA in the 1930s, to the domain of the TreePeople.

Dearing Mountain Trail descends east a half-mile to Iredell Lane. Walk down the cul de sac 150 feet or so and you'll spot the beginning of the upper length of Dearing Mountain Trail. (See Fryman Canyon hike.) Continue down the lane to Iredell Street to Fryman Road and back to the trailhead.

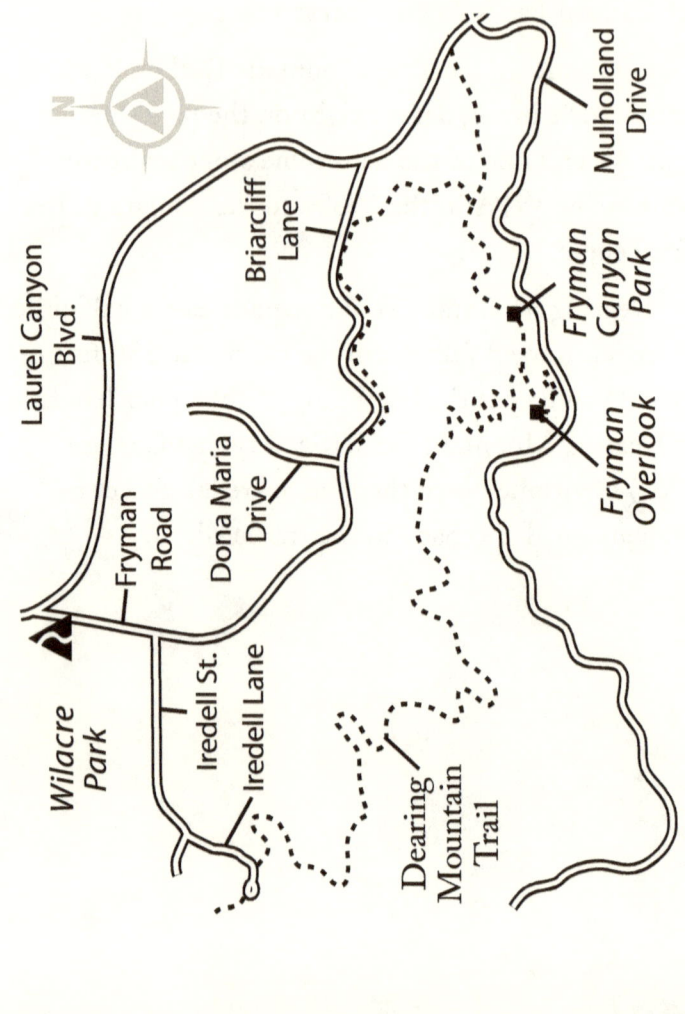

FRYMAN OVERLOOK

DEARING MOUNTAIN TRAIL

From Wilacre Park to Fryman Overlook is 4 miles round trip with 500-foot gain

Fryman Overlook offers the urban mountaineer great clear-day vistas of the San Fernando Valley. Smog-free views also include the Verdugo, Santa Susana and San Gabriel mountain ranges.

On this exploration via footpaths and suburban streets, the hiker experiences a section of Hollywood Hills heavily altered by the hands of humans. Hillsides have been planted in all manner of native and exotic trees and plants and terraced to create pads for the construction of homes. The hiker looks out at some truly astonishing and seemingly precarious residences, including homes on stilts and homes built stair-step-like down precipitous canyon walls.

I prefer beginning this hike at Wilacre Park and doing an out-and-back on Dearing Mountain Trail up to Fryman Canyon Overlook on Mulholland

Drive. But there are options: you can begin the hike at the overlook and you can make a loop with a combo of trail and road-walking.

DIRECTIONS: From the Ventura Freeway (101) in Studio City, exit on Laurel Canyon Boulevard and drive south 1.5 miles to Fryman Canyon Road. Turn right and park immediately in the lot of Wilacre Park (fee).

THE HIKE: Walk south on Fryman Road to Iredell Street, turn right and follow it east. The street bends south into Iredell Lane. About a half mile from the trailhead and shortly before the end of the cul-de-sac, look left for a yellow gate and the beginning of Dearing Mountain Trail.

Climb steps and begin a short, but steep ascent up a terraced slope. Shaded by towering eucalyptus and native oaks, the trail descends to the head of a ravine that's watered by a seasonal creek. The trail then ascends moderately with the help of switchbacks up the chaparral-covered south wall of Fryman Canyon to Mulholland Drive and Fryman Overlook.

Enjoy the far-reaching vistas and pause at displays to learn about the inspiration for scenic Mulholland Drive and about Betty P. Dearing (1917-1977) and her efforts to "create a nature walk from Los Angeles to the sea."

Return option: Walk a short distance on Dearing Mountain Trail to a junction; instead of descending the way you came, keep straight and follow the sage- and toyon-lined path as it heads east below Mulholland Drive. About 0.4 mile from the overlook, you'll ignore a right-forking trail leading up to Laurel Canyon Boulevard, and stick with the main trail that turns north then east again and descending to junction a dirt fire road. Head left (downhill) on the road 0.25 mile to the bottom of the canyon to paved road. Join a sometimes sketchy footpath on the left for 300 feet or so, return to the road, head left, and descend to the corner of Dona Maria Drive and Fryman Road. Follow Fryman Road back to the trailhead at Wilacre Park.

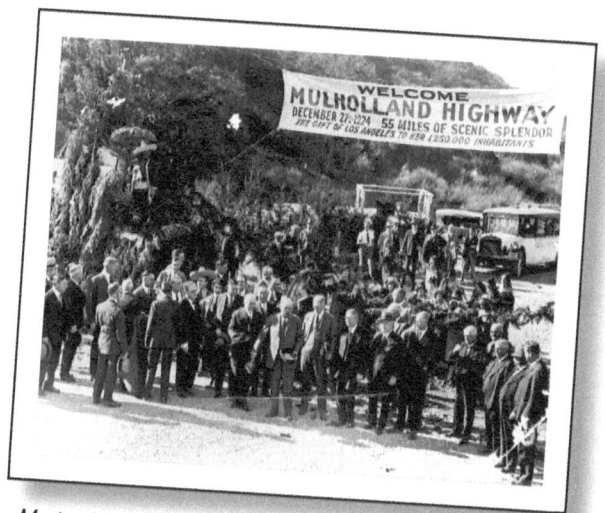

Motorists have been using Mulholland to reach parks and hiking trails for nearly a century.

Dixie Canyon Park

Thank you, Warren Beatty. The actor donated a lovely woodland perched in the hills above the San Fernando Valley for a park in 1986.

Dixie Canyon Park is a 20-acre preserve of coast live oak and black walnut with a perennial creek. Given the small size of the park and its short trail (a half-mile partial loop), you probably won't want to travel much out of your way to visit it. Nevertheless if you're looking for a quick getaway from nearby Ventura Boulevard or in the vicinity—that is to say, hiking larger parklands around Coldwater Canyon and Mulholland Drive—drop in on Dixie Canyon.

From the trailhead, you take a flight of stairs, walk along a creek, and enter the shady canyon. You'd think a trail that begins at a cul de sac surrounded by hillside townhouses would be in better shape, but over the years I've always observed the path to be kind of washed out and crowded by poison oak.

On the upside, it can be a surprisingly wet and wild walk through this island of greenery. Dixie Canyon doesn't attract a crowd, that's for sure, and you might just have the whole park to yourself for your 15 to 20 minute hike.

DIRECTIONS: From the Ventura Freeway (101) exit on Woodman Avenue and head south 0.5 mile to Ventura Boulevard. Turn left and drive 0.2 mile east to Dixie Canyon Avenue. Turn right (south) and proceed 0.75 mile; when the avenue bends right, turn left on Dixie Canyon Road and travel 0.25 mile to the narrow road's end and entrance to Dixie Canyon Park. Parking (scarce) is located along the road.

Stairway to a little haven: Dixie Canyon

Briar Summit Open Space Preserve

Views from the 1,500-foot Briar Summit are impressive and far-reaching—as the military recognized in the 1960s when it built a Nike Missile observation platform atop the peak. Reward for a short walk in what is now Briar Summit Open Spacre Preserve is a sweeping vista: the entire San Fernando Valley, Verdugo Mountains, San Gabriel Mountains, miles and miles of freeways and the Los Angeles River.

The view takes in the tall buildings where the film industry is headquartered—a reminder of just how much "Hollywood" is in the Valley, including Universal Studios Disney Studios, Warner Brothers Studios. You can't miss the tallest building around, emblazoned with its company names: Comcast- NBC- Universal. From Briar Summit, you get the same (or better) stunning view as that from the official Universal City Overlook on Mulholland Drive, minus the traffic and crowds.

Briar Summit Open Space Preserve

Thwarting two decades worth of efforts by developers to build hillside haciendas on the slopes of this landmark mountain, the Santa Monica Mountains Conservancy succeeded in preserving Briar Summit as parkland in 2004. The 52-acre open space preserve is part of a chain of natural areas intended to serve as corridors for wildlife traveling to and fro from the eastern Santa Monica Mountains/Hollywood Hills to Griffith Park. Wildlife sightings on Briar Mountain include deer, fox, bobcats, coyote, rabbits, and quail.

The short hike (0.8 mile round trip with 250 feet in elevation gain) on a paved L.A. Department of Water & Power road begins with a mellow 0.25 mile-ascent to a large turnout. Enjoy views down into Laurel Canyon. For an additional perspective, take the short dirt side trail onto a nearby ridge.

Continue the climb to a water tank, and perch for panoramic views. Radio towers mark the gated end of the road, the end of the hike. Cement stairs lead to the true Briar Summit, which is topped by a small antenna.

DIRECTIONS: From Highway 101 in Studio City, exit on Laurel Canyon Blvd. and drive south (toward Studio City) 2.8 miles to Mulholland Drive. Turn left and very soon turn right on Briar Summit Drive. At a road split in 0.1 mile, stay left to keep on Briar Summit Drive, which leads another 0.3 mile or so to Briar Summit Open Space Preserve. Roadside parking is available below the preserve.

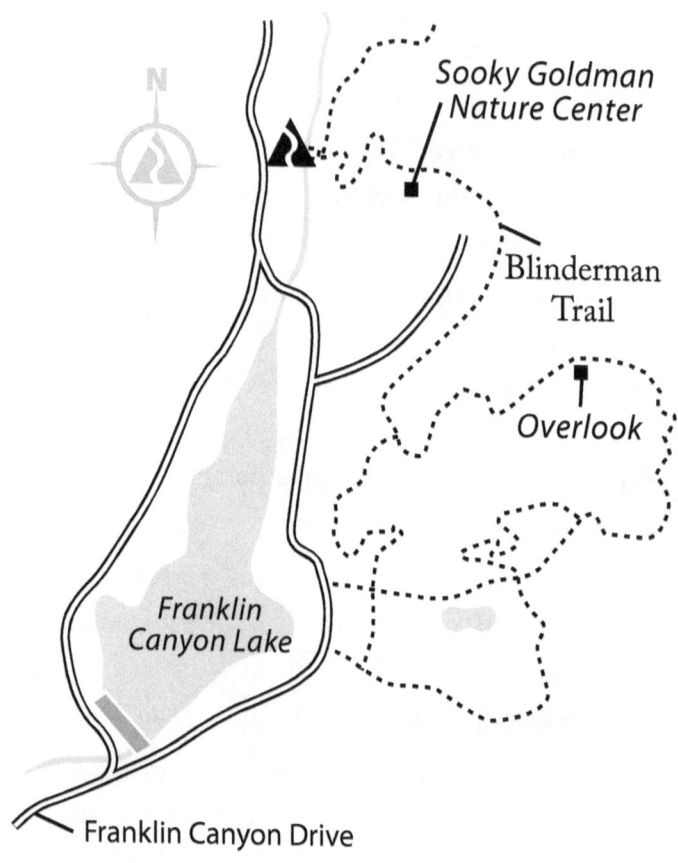

Upper Franklin Canyon

Blinderman Trail

From Sooky Goldman Nature Center, 1.5 mile loop with 200-foot elevation gain

It's appeared on your TV a hundred times, but you probably don't know its name. Television producers and moviemakers have found Franklin Canyon to be a convincing substitute for a wide variety of locales ranging from High Sierra forest to jungle lagoon. Check at the visitor center for a list of TV shows, films and commercials—classic and contemporary—that have been filmed in this preserve in Beverly Hills.

Franklin Canyon on most days offers hikers, birdwatchers and nature lovers a tranquil retreat. Administered by the Mountains Recreation & Conservation Authority, the 605-acre preserve is part of Santa Monica Mountains National Recreation Area.

Franklin Canyon's William O. Douglas Outdoor Classroom helps young people connect with nature as does Sooky Goldman Nature Center. A trail named for conservationist Barbara Blinderman heads into the hills behind the nature center and offers an intro to the charms of Franklin Canyon. The zigzagging, stair-stepping path connects to other short trails.

Upper canyon highlight Franklin Reservoir was constructed in 1910, then improved and expanded in the 1930s. After a 1971 earthquake, the earthen dam was declared unsafe, so the reservoir is no longer part of the Southland's far-reaching waterworks system. Today the reservoir—now more lyrically referred to as Franklin Lake—is home to bass, catfish, ducks and coots. The lake is an important stopover for migratory birds.

Combine the short hillside hike on Blinderman Trail with a pleasant walk of just a little less than a mile around the lake.

DIRECTIONS: In Studio City, exit the Ventura Freeway (101) on Coldwater Canyon Drive. Head south 2.5 miles to a hilltop meeting with Mulholland Drive. With TreePeople Headquarters on your left, make a hard right on Franklin Canyon Drive and proceed 0.75 mile to the Sooky Goldman Nature Center parking lot.

THE HIKE: From the parking lot, hike over the small wooden bridge to meet the trail. Cross Mountain Trail leads north to Coldwater Canyon Park while you step up the hill to Sooky Goldman Nature Center and cross the courtyard to meet signed Blinderman Trail.

The trail soon forks. Stay right and follow the path to meet an unsigned path on the left. Leave Blinderman Trail and ascend this path to a vista point, then to two more, each offering a differing perspective on the canyon and Franklin Lake.

(From this third vista point, you can descend east on a steep path to the bottom of a ravine, go right and loop back to meet Blindnerman Trail.)

Retracing your steps to Blinderman Trail, head south to the canyon floor and a dirt road. Go left, passing ephemeral Wild Pond. Another brief stair-stepping path goes up and down the slope to the north. At the four-way junction, head into the eucalyptus grove, traveling south then west on the trail to the park road. Walk Franklin Canyon Drive or the path beside the lake back to the nature center and trailhead.

Nature and nurture in Franklin Canyon

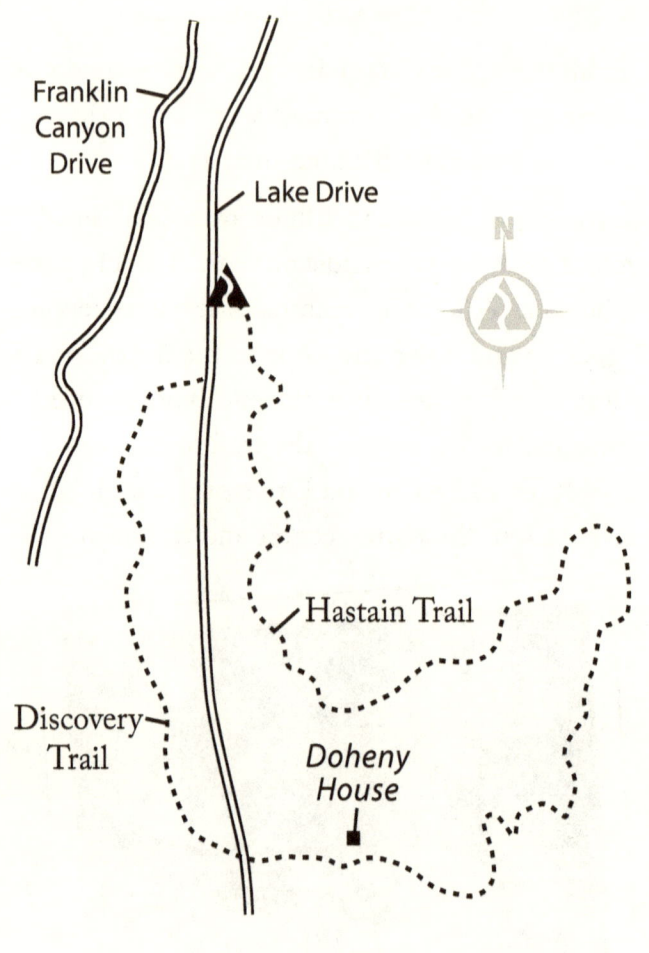

Lower Franklin Canyon
Hastain, Discovery Trails

2.2-mile loop with 500-foot elevation gain

Hastain Trail explores the lower part of Franklin Canyon. It ascends the eastern ridge of the canyon and offers fine views of the San Fernando Valley, Beverly Hills, the busy Wilshire corridor, and much more.

It's a favorite hike in the hood for residents of that famed zip code 90210, Beverly Hills, and from surrounding communities on both the Valley side and Westside of L.A. The loop is a good workout; however, if you want to cut it short, you can opt for a 1.8 mile loop with a 300-foot elevation gain

A few years ago, the popular trail, long beloved by hikers, was the center of a heated controversy and legal dispute when a homeowner fenced off the trail and denied passage across his property. It seems real estate developer Mohamed Hadid, who has designed and built more than a dozen Ritz-Carlton hotels plus many Beverly Hills mansions, owns 97 acres right next to Franklin Canyon Park and a short length of Hastain Trail crosses his property. Eventually, conservationists gained a public easement for the trail and it was re-opened.

As if the vistas on this hike aren't reason enough to take this hike, you'll also get the opportunity to admire outcroppings of Santa Monica slate, the oldest rock in the Hollywood Hills/Santa Monica Mountains. Pretty exciting, huh? The slate is geological evidence that the mountains were once beneath the ocean.

DIRECTIONS: In Studio City, exit the Ventura Freeway (101) on Coldwater Canyon Drive. Head south 2.5 miles to a hilltop meeting with Mulholland Drive. With TreePeople Headquarters on your left, make a hard right on Franklin Canyon Drive and proceed 1.3 miles. Bear left onto Lake Drive and continue another 0.3 mile to the well-signed Hastain trailhead on the left and roadside parking

From the Westside/Beverly Hills, take Sunset Boulevard to Beverly Drive and head north for 1.2 miles. Turn right onto Franklin Canyon Drive and drive a mile to Lake Drive. Turn right and reach the trailhead and parking in 0.3 mile.

THE HIKE: Ascend the wide fire road (signed Hastain Trail) across sage- and chamise-covered slopes on the east side of the canyon. Pass a junction with a footpath on your left (a return route) 0.4 mile from the start, and hike through a gate at the 0.7 mile mark.

A mile out, reach an overlook and enjoy West L.A. and Santa Monica Bay vistas. (You can cut the hike short here by descending on a footpath to the right.) Continue on Hastain Trail, which continues to climb along the canyon's east ridge.

The trail tops out about 1.3 miles from the start. Say adios to the fire road, which leads toward some haciendas. Instead, descend the steep, narrow footpath, which drops 400 feet in elevation in 0.5 mile before depositing you back on Hastain Trail. Retrace your steps back to the trailhead.

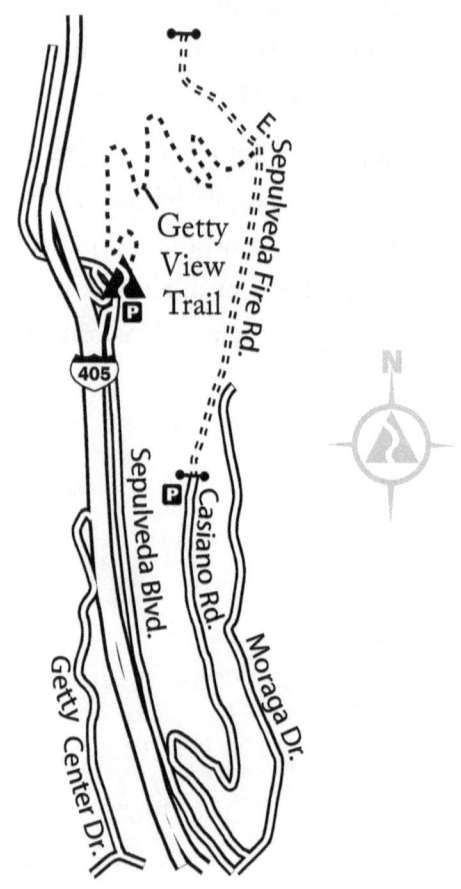

BEL-AIR

GETTY VIEW TRAIL

From Sepulveda Boulevard to East Sepulveda Fire Road is 2.5 miles round trip with 500-foot elevation gain; to Casiano Road is 3.5 miles round trip

Located just 12 miles from downtown Los Angeles, Bel-Air is an uber-wealth residential enclave long popular with celebs and entertainment industry movers and shakers. One way to view Bel-Air is take a drive through its grand entrance gates off Sunset Boulevard and tour along windy lanes past luxe mansions and their elegantly landscaped grounds.

Another way to view Bel-Air is to take a hike in the hills above it. Getty View Trail leads to a great vista of a trio of upscale Westside communities known as the Three Bs: Bel-Air, Beverly Hills and Brentwood.

And Getty View Trail gives you more: a great view of Getty Center (that grand art center and one of the most popular museums in the U.S) and famed Sepulveda Pass.

The view of the pass has changed immeasurably since the 1840s when Francisco Sepulveda rode through this gap in the eastern Santa Monica Mountains and over his 30,000-acre Rancho San Vicente y Santa Monica. The pass, a boulevard (the longest road in both the city and county of Los Angeles), and many more features were named for the Sepulvedas, major 19th-century Southern California landowners.

The path is surely one of the most freeway-convenient in the Southland. Instead of idling along in heavy traffic, frustrated commuters could exit on Sepulveda and take a hike. From the top of the trail, hikers can gather their own traffic reports; the view of the San Diego Freeway rivals that of what a helicopter news crew can see.

When that San Diego Freeway Sig-Alert ends, return to civilization, such as it is. Getty View Trail switchbacks up the brushy slopes east of Sepulveda Pass to meet dirt East Sepulveda Fire Road. Such fire roads are crucial to fire-fighting efforts in the steep terrain surrounding Bel-Air's pricey real estate. On November 6, 1961, a wind-driven wildfire destroyed 484 homes. On December 6, 2017, a fire started in a homeless camp burned hillsides in the same area as the 1961 conflagration, though fortunately only 6 homes were lost.

Getty View Trail delivers on the promise of its name at its south end. Other views from the ridge-hugging fire road include the Santa Monica

Mountains, San Gabriel Mountains, the Wilshire corridor and the Pacific Ocean.

Views the trail delivers; peace it does not. Given the path's proximity to the freeway, tranquility would be too much to ask of this trail, so don't. At times, trailside traffic noise is as intense as anything experienced as a motorist in the lanes below.

DIRECTIONS: From the San Diego Freeway, take the Getty Center exit and follow the signs directing you down Sepuleveda Boulevard. Just as Sepulveda crosses under the San Diego Freeway, look left for the signed Getty Center Trail and parking area. The landscaped trailhead includes picnic tables and interpretive kiosks.

THE HIKE: The path ascends past a few handsome sycamores (the only shade en route) and climbs northeast. The powerful din of the freeway seems to vibrate the very landscape. Switchback by switchback, more and more of Sepulveda Pass is revealed.

Getty View Trail tops out on a ridgeline where it meets wide, dirt East Sepulveda Fire Road. A quarter-mile hike north on the fire road leads to its end at a private residential area.

Hike south on the fire road and soon get grand views to the west of Getty Center, and a surprising view to the east of undeveloped Hoag Canyon. Did Sepulveda Canyon once resemble this nearly pristine canyon? The fire road ends in a half mile at Casiano Road on the far west side of Bel-Air.

TRAILMASTERSTORE.COM

All of John McKinney's books including,
Hike the Santa Monica Mountains,
are available from The Trailmaster Store.

THETRAILMASTER.COM

- Tips
- Tours
- Trails
- Tales

JOHN MCKINNEY

John McKinney is the author of 30 books about hiking, parklands and nature, including *Hiking on the Edge: Dreams, Schemes, and 1600 Miles on the California Coastal Trail.*

HIKE Santa Barbara and *HIKE Griffith Park* are among the titles in the The Trailmaster's "Best Day Hikes" series, designed to give hikers the information they need in an engaging and easily accessible way.

For 18 years, he wrote a weekly hiking column for the *Los Angeles Times*, and has hiked and enthusiastically described more than ten thousand miles of trail across America and around the world. John, a.k.a. The Trailmaster, has written more than a thousand articles about hiking plus numerous trail guidebooks in his "Best Day Hikes" series, including regional bestsellers, *HIKE Southern California* and *Day Hiker's Guide to California's State Parks.*

A passionate advocate for hiking and our need to reconnect with nature, John McKinney shares his expertise on radio, TV, online, and as a public speaker.

JOHN MCKINNEY
"EVERY TRAIL TELLS A STORY."

HIKE ON.

TheTrailmaster.com

www.ingramcontent.com/pod-product-compliance
Lightning Source LLC
Chambersburg PA
CBHW030444300426
44112CB00009B/1163